Praise for
The Retention Revolution

People don't just quit bad jobs and bad bosses—they leave toxic cultures. In the wake of the Great Resignation, Erica Keswin offers an engaging, practical look at how to build a workplace where current employees want to stay and those who have left can't wait to come back.

—ADAM GRANT
#1 *New York Times* bestselling author of *Think Again* and *Hidden Potential*, and host of the TED podcast *WorkLife*

Once again, Erica has given us the book every leader needs to read. The third in her "human trilogy," Erica's insightful, accessible, timely book revolutionizes our thoughts about retention and the power of human connection.

—KATIE COURIC
journalist and bestselling author

I can't think of a better way to embrace the long game than to completely reframe the way we think about work postpandemic. In *The Retention Revolution*, Erica Keswin demonstrates that people-first best practices create a virtuous cycle for all stakeholders.

—DORIE CLARK
Wall Street Journal bestselling author of
The Long Game and executive education faculty,
Duke University Fuqua School of Business

Vulnerability at work is here to stay. And while we're all still figuring out exactly what that looks like in the workplace, Erica Keswin's book *The Retention Revolution* makes it clear that people want to express themselves, feel respected, and bring their full human selves to work. This book is for any leader wanting to invest in their people—yes, even with all the big feelings that come with them.

—LIZ FOSSLIEN and MOLLIE WEST DUFFY
coauthors of the *Wall Street Journal* bestseller
*No Hard Feelings: The Secret Power of Embracing
Emotions at Work* and *Big Feelings: How to
Be Okay When Things Are Not Okay*

The Retention Revolution lays out the best ideas and the coolest innovations in management that came out of the pandemic period. A must-read for staying ahead of the curve.

—PETER CAPPELLI
George W. Taylor Professor of Management; director,
Center for Human Resources The Wharton School;
and professor of Education University of Pennsylvania

For decades we've held a collective story about what work should look like. But recent years and events have shown us that the old story was keeping us stuck in a vicious cycle that didn't really serve anyone. Erica Keswin's book *The Retention Revolution* asks us to rewrite the story of work and life. This book shows us how to move through the growing pains of change to reimagine a world of work that better serves all stakeholders, creating a virtuous cycle. And it all starts with empathy and connection.

—LORI GOTTLIEB
New York Times bestselling author of *Maybe You
Should Talk to Someone* and cohost of
the *Dear Therapists* podcast

The Retention Revolution shows us why we need to put the human back into our retention strategies and provides practical guidance that companies can use to keep current and past employees connected in ways that benefit the organization, its people, and society.

—JEN FISHER
Wall Street Journal bestselling author of
Work Better Together and chief
well-being officer, Deloitte

Postpandemic, leaders and employers have been reminded of the human condition and that prioritizing DEI, well-being, and employee education and development are table stakes. As Erica Keswin so aptly points out in her book *The Retention Revolution*, we have to reimagine our relationship with our employees to one of connection, support, and trust. We need to create an experience that allows employees to be and become their best—even if it means the programs we offer develop them right out the door!

The Retention Revolution is a smart guide for leaders who get it—because they know that their people will create value at their current companies and beyond.

—MARISSA ANDRADA
former chief people officer, Chipotle; board director,
Krispy Kreme; and host of *Culture Cast*

During Covid, we all had to recalculate our work and lives as our world was turned upside down. But the pandemic also gave us an opportunity to recalculate our very assumptions about work itself, especially at a time when we have five different generations navigating this new world of work. In her book *The Retention Revolution* Erica Keswin asks leaders to let go of old ideas that don't serve anyone anymore and instead bravely embrace new ways of working that work for all.

—LINDSEY POLLAK
New York Times bestselling author of *The Remix: How to Lead and Succeed in the Multigenerational Workplace*

The pandemic saw a record number of women leave the workforce due to caregiving responsibilities that overwhelmingly fall on women. And we haven't seen a full recovery since. Smart leaders, as Erica Keswin shares in her book *The Retention Revolution*, will make flexibility a core pillar of their workplace, no matter the ups and downs of the economy. Because smart leaders know that making work more equitable, inclusive, and fair is good for business. Smart leaders will read this book today!

—EVE RODSKY
New York Times bestselling author of *Fair Play*

Succeeding as a founder is tough, and the odds are stacked against you. But building a truly human workplace while you grow your startup is a smart way to create a competitive advantage. In her book *The Retention Revolution* Erica Keswin reframes key ideas about how we work, which leaders in any company—from startups to multinational conglomerates—can embrace and implement.

—ALISA COHN
executive coach and author of
From Start-Up to Grown-Up

To succeed in the new, ever-changing world of work, every leader needs to reevaluate what work means, what workplaces are even for, and how we connect with our people. In *The Retention Revolution*, Erica Keswin makes a clear case for prioritizing and honoring our relationships with employees— and sharp advice for how to do that—in order to cultivate an environment of trust and retain our best talent.

—AMY GALLO
author of *Getting Along: How to Work with
Anyone (Even Difficult People)* and
contributing editor, *Harvard Business Review*

THE
RETENTION
REVOLUTION

THE
RETENTION
REVOLUTION

7 Surprising (and Very Human!) Ways to Keep Employees Connected to Your Company

Erica Keswin

New York Chicago San Francisco Athens London Madrid
Mexico City Milan New Delhi Singapore Sydney Toronto

1 2 3 4 5 6 7 8 9   LCR   28 27 26 25 24 23

ISBN   978-1-265-15868-2
MHID   1-265-15868-1

e-ISBN   978-1-265-15912-2
e-MHID   1-265-15912-2

McGraw Hill books are available at special quantity discounts to use as premiums and sales promotions or for use in corporate training programs. To contact a representative, please visit the Contact Us pages at www .mhprofessional.com.

McGraw Hill is committed to making our products accessible to all learners. To learn more about the available support and accommodations we offer, please contact us at accessibility@mheducation.com. We also participate in the Access Text Network (www.accesstext.org), and ATN members may submit requests through ATN.

This book is dedicated to the men and women on the front lines of the Covid pandemic, and for their brave work in one of the most challenging workplaces in human history. Thank you for making this book—and our lives—possible.

CONTENTS

Preface ix

INTRODUCTION   Isn't It Ironic?   1

CHAPTER ONE   Start as You Mean to Go Onboarding   11

CHAPTER TWO   Say Goodbye to the Lifestyles of the Rich and Flexible and Hello to Flex for All   35

CHAPTER THREE   There Is No Curtain: *The Case for Human Professionalism*   69

CHAPTER FOUR   We Have to Stop Meeting Like This: *The Three P's of Meetings*   91

CHAPTER FIVE   From Ladders to Lily Pads: *Learning and Development for the Human Professional*   123

CHAPTER SIX   Managers Are Having a Moment: *Why You Should Invest in Your Most Valuable Employees*   155

CHAPTER SEVEN   Offboarding as You Mean to
Go On (and On)   175

EPILOGUE   It's Not You. It's Not Me. It's Us.   203

Acknowledgments   209

Notes   211

Index   243

PREFACE

I have a confession to make.

This isn't really a book about retention. What I mean is, it's not *not* about retention, but retention might not be what you think it is.

Please allow me to explain.

When I started thinking about this book in 2021, I, like everyone else, was still reeling as we'd watched the mass exodus from physical offices into people's home offices, living rooms, and closets, with kids and dogs on laps and spouses in the background reaching into the fridge. It seems like a long time ago now, I realize. But I believe that we'll continue to learn all kinds of lessons from that historic time—yes, even as we might be clenching our teeth in the short term.

In March 2020, for many of my friends and colleagues, working from home started off as a welcome break from the commute and travel. But it didn't take long for it to get old. Whole families under one roof, parents working, homeschooling, once happily single people plummeted into extreme isolation—it's no wonder that along with our Wi-Fi crashing, our mental health did as well. The US Census

Household Pulse Survey reported that during the first year of the pandemic, "Moderate to severe anxiety peaked at 37.3 percent of the adult population during the pandemic, up from 6.9 percent in 2019, and moderate to severe depression among adults jumped from 7.0 percent to 30.2 percent over the pandemic."[1]

My family wasn't completely unscathed, but relatively lucky. My mom died at the beginning of the lockdown, which was painful and strange; the pandemic will forever be part of my generational DNA.

After sharing a home office with my husband for 16 months, I have a new appreciation for something a childhood friend shared—her grandmother told her grandfather after they retired, "Honey, I love you, but not for lunch." And that was on a good day. (Have we ever been so frustrated by the fact that people *breathe*?) But we made it. Today, the kids have all flown the coop for college. My husband and I are back in our own lanes and having lunch together on the weekends.

Friends of mine—especially women with small kids—had more at stake.

I remember speaking to a friend with an Ivy League education and a big job in tech about how every morning she helped her five-year-old log on to virtual kindergarten and found only moms and caregivers helping the kids with online school, even if both parents worked. As she described the scene, I could see the writing on the walls: many women would begin to opt out of the workforce. And opt out, they did.

As of September 2022, women's labor force participation rate was 58.4 percent, compared to 59.2 percent just prior to the pandemic. "That means the U.S. labor force has lost 1.067 million women since February 2020."[2] And an even more depressing stat to consider: "Women have added $2 trillion to the US economy since 1970 by increasing their labor force participation. The pandemic has siphoned off 63% of that progress, or *$1.26 trillion worth of economic potential.*"[3] (emphasis mine)

Wow.

It wasn't long before my head was spinning as we all watched people quit their jobs in droves, inspiring panic and despair in leaders across industries. Starting in June 2021, the US Bureau of Labor Statistics has reported over four million (non-farm) resignations *every* month since (as of January 2023).[4]

Incredible.

In an attempt to stop the bleeding, leaders relied on what they knew and then found some tricks up their sleeves none of us knew existed: signing bonuses for bus drivers and workers at Burger King, four-day workweeks, Starbucks home deliveries, total flexibility.

They didn't know it yet, but we were in the midst of what has been referred to as "The Great Resignation" by Texas A&M professor Anthony Klotz. A 2022 search for the term turned up more than 232 million references at such household name sites as BBC, NPR, *Forbes*, and dictionary.com.[5] And leaders were scrambling.

The Great Resignation. The Great Reevaluation. The Great Reshuffle. The Great Do-Over. Whatever you call it, the shift in hiring loomed large for people around the world, as well as my clients. The writer in me watched closely as headlines like "Talent Is Winning the War" filled my news feed.

Across the board and industries, people demanded to be treated like human beings and leaders had no choice but to listen.

As someone who wrote a book called *Bring Your Human to Work* in 2018, I was listening, too. And taking notes.

As I spoke to clients who were quickly trying to react and address these changes, I began to realize that I had a front seat to something historic. I knew the workplace would never be the same. It was exciting, and I was inspired.

And then, just as we began to see a new beginning take shape—people- and digital-first organizations in late 2022, leaders were hit with a new kind of panic: companies were hit with rounds and rounds of layoffs, inflation, a looming recession, and market volatility—insecurity as far as the eye could see.

New headlines started popping up. From the *Wall Street Journal*: "Tech Workers Face a New Reality as Talent Wars Turn to Pink Slips,"[6] and "As White-Collar Layoffs Rise, Blue-Collar Resilience Faces Test in 2023."[7] From the *New York Times*: "Getting Rid of Remote Work Will Take More Than a Downturn,"[8] and from Bloomberg: "US Employees Say They're Losing the Upper Hand as Layoffs Mount."[9]

Were the tables turning like the pundits and journalists predicted?

Would The Great Resignation become the "Not-So-Great Back to Business as Usual"?

Turns out that in 2023, yes, while tech took a beating during what seemed like the downturn of Q4 in 2022 and Q1 of 2023, there were over 10 million jobs open[10] and only 5.7 million people unemployed.[11] That's almost two job openings for every job seeker.

As a Gen Xer who has been in the people space for over 25 years, this was not my first rodeo. I worked as an executive recruiter in the early 2000s during the dot-com crash, which eliminated more than a million jobs.[12] And then, fast-forward to 2008. I was once again on the front lines, counseling leaders through unexpected layoffs in my job as a career coach at the NYU Stern School of Business. This is the cycle of business. It's not easy, but the pendulum always swings one way and then the other.

And this is where I want to share the one lesson I've learned watching this whole thing unfold. It's bigger than the expected expansions and contractions in the job market, and I believe it will have lasting impacts long after the Covid crisis has been written into the history books.

In the so-called "war for talent," *everyone* loses.

I know it might not seem like much, but the very notion of employees and employers on opposite sides of the bargaining table is breaking down, to everyone's benefit. Instead, successful companies understand that employees are actually your most important stakeholder—your most valued customer, in fact. Leaders can't horde employees; instead, people must be treated with respect and dignity, which may include supporting them as they move on.

The fact of the matter is, the revolving door of talent is not a problem. In fact, quite the opposite! When you learn how to harness all that energy, what you get is a virtuous cycle of robust opportunity. And then your whole perspective shifts from trying to keep people in their chairs to understanding how important it is to help people learn and develop and evolve, even if it means they're working for someone else.

Which is to say, when I started this book back in 2022, I, like everyone else, wanted to know why so many people were quitting, and what companies could do to bring people back. And I, like everyone else, thought we could solve the problem of retention if we could just find the perfect cocktail of benefits and perks.

I quickly discovered that I was asking the wrong question, especially the "How can we bring them back?" part. We're *way* beyond any superficial solutions.

And I still believe it.

As soon as I started unpacking the very idea of retention, I realized we had to reframe everything we thought we knew about how work *works*.

That's why the very concept of retention is changing.

That's why this is a Retention *Revolution*. And it's not really even about retention anymore, though it's not *not* about retention, either.

It's all about meeting people where they are, as they are, for as long as they choose to stay connected—which will hopefully be long after they leave.

This is a new, very human, very real world, and there's no going back.

ISN'T IT IRONIC?

OLD IDEA:

Stability leads to growth.

NEW BEGINNING:

Dynamic change powers the ecosystem of
today's workplace.

Everyone knows that in order for anything to develop
well—children, books, ideas, markets, companies—the
chaos must be tamed.

Right?

I mean, doesn't stability lead to growth?

Well, not necessarily.

In fact, when we look more closely at how progress
actually happens, we can see that instability is not just an
important part—but a *necessary* part—of the process.

Let's take a look at the topsy-turvy world of employment
over the past few years. Data from the US Bureau of Labor
Statistics show that as of January 2022, the average tenure
of a US worker is about 4.1 years, as compared to 4.6 in
2014.[13] And according to career-planning site Zippia, "65%
of American workers are actively searching for a new full-
time job right now."[14] On top of that, we've seen the highest
quit rates since the 1960s and 1970s.[15]

This turbulence is certainly bumpy in the immediate for
many, but also filled with potential in the long term for the
whole. To wit—since 2020, the United States has seen an
unprecedented rise in new businesses. In fact, according to
the US Chamber of Commerce, the United States has seen

"the largest increase in new business applications in recorded history."[16] Specifically, more than "4.3 million new business applications were filed in 2020, an increase of 24% over 2019."[17] So much so that experts like John Lettieri, a cofounder of the Economic Innovation Group (EIG), reports that he and his colleagues were "doing this mutual head-scratching, like, *What is happening? Is this going to last? . . .* and things kept on taking off."[18]

As *Atlantic* writer Annie Lowrey puts it, the past few years have seen what she calls "creative destruction" at play—the exact opposite of stability at all costs. She writes, "Covid-19 killed countless businesses. Surprisingly, it also launched a whole bunch of new ones,"[19] which is not entirely due to predictable measures, like different sectors being affected by lockdowns or the economics of government stimuli. She explains:

> The coronavirus destroyed brick-and-mortar restaurants but boosted spending on delivery; it killed gyms and yoga studios but increased interest in personal fitness equipment; it decimated formal office-wear sales but boosted revenue for skin care and loungewear; it halted business travel but led to the uptake of virtual-conferencing and collaborative-work technologies.[20]

When the ground is turned up, growth is possible.

Now, of course losses are painful, there's no denying that. And there's no doubt that short-term hires and turnover are expensive—to the individual company at least—anywhere from half up to a whopping *two times* an employee's salary.[21] But if we zoom out to look at the big picture, we can see how a failure in one area can very well lead to success in another.

And how one company's ex-employee just might be the world's next best entrepreneur.

In the Retention Revolution, if we play our cards right from the moment we make contact with the people on our teams, that very same ex-employee can continue to be an asset as a company's referral source, brand ambassador, and maybe even a boomerang employee. Not to mention, their new venture just might solve one of our biggest problems or provide a service that enhances our lives.

In other words, because our time with employees is increasingly short, we need to reconceive talent as just one part of our long-game strategy.

As former head of HR at LinkedIn and author Steve Cadigan puts it, "Higher turnover builds more extensive networks, and greater network traffic enables the exchange of more intelligence and ideas."[22]

Indeed.

In the Retention Revolution, we transform employee churn into a positive return. Rather than a desperate attempt to retain people by keeping them chained to their desks with golden handcuffs, the Retention Revolution means we lean into recognizing the future as an open ecosystem of opportunity—a virtuous cycle.

After all, since the very definition of *retain* is to "keep," "hold on to," or "possess," we know that goal is misguided. Clearly, we can't control employees. We can't control anyone! Nor should we. Our lives and companies will always be in flux; change is the one constant.

And isn't it ironic?

As I will describe in this book, when you accept change, your business has a much better chance of lasting. When you support a commitment to your employees' individual growth, commitment to your company just might follow; when you help employees connect with their own purpose, your company thrives.

As a bona fide control freak, I get it! The chaos seems scary. Especially in business.

And that's why I wrote this book—to help you shift your point of view and see how every end has the potential to be a new beginning. *The Retention Revolution: 7 Surprising (and Very Human!) Ways to Keep Employees Connected to Your Company* is the paradigm-shifting guide for brave leaders ready to see some of their most fundamental assumptions about work in a new light—one that can support and inspire a truly human workplace.

Specifically, we will dismantle seven old ideas about work and then rebuild them into new beginnings.

These seven old ideas are:

1. Onboarding is the thing you do before the "real" work begins. (In fact, you only have one chance to make a first impression and boy, will it last, and last, and last . . .)
2. Employees are only working when you can see them. (It's official: autonomy and flexibility make work *work*.)
3. "Human professional" is an oxymoron. (Blending vulnerability and professionalism is a hallmark of today's workplace.)
4. Meetings are just . . . what you do. (In fact, they can be much fewer and far between, and fun!)
5. Professional development should be job-related. (The reality is, companies benefit so much from employees who are deeply connected in their lives that personal development *is* professional development.)

6. Managers are in the messy middle of their career and your organization—and are easily overlooked. (Today, they're your MVP.)

7. There's the door. Don't let it hit you. . . . (The Retention Revolution says goodbye to such black-and-white, linear thinking and celebrates the virtuous cycle.)

And that's not all.

We'll explore important themes, aspects of the revolution that need to be integrated in everything a human leader does. For instance, instead of limiting diversity, equity, and inclusion to one chapter, I've incorporated elements of diversity, equity, and inclusion (DEI) throughout. Today, we know that a business cannot be successful if people don't feel like they belong. It's time to move this critical work from the margins of our thinking to the center.

I'll also explore the way our beliefs about technology have changed. We used to think that tech is like money—more is always better. Today, we know that throwing technology at a problem—or money for that matter—is so before times. Every chapter has a Tech Box that highlights companies and/ or products that have successfully found the "sweet spot" between tech and connect.

There's never been a more confusing time to be in business. That's why I've written *The Retention Revolution* for all leaders, especially those I've met since March 2020, the ones who were stressed to the max dealing with what social psychologist Dr. Amy Cuddy calls the "pandemic flux syndrome"—that anxious, not-knowing-what's-next feeling we all experienced at one time or another. But the Retention Revolution is bigger than a pandemic. Yes, I'll take what we've learned and operationalize it for the future, using concrete science and stories from companies that have thrived in the past three years. But more than just a response to this moment in our cultural timeline, the Retention Revolution will improve our companies and our lives under any condition.

It's true that leaders, employers, journalists, and experts have been pointing to this talent upheaval as one of the biggest challenges companies have ever faced. Perhaps, it's also an opportunity to put to rest some old ideas about work that no longer serve us, starting with the assumption that turnover is bad or permanent or represents a closed door. Nothing could be further from the truth!

The Muse, an online career platform, surveyed 2,500 US adults and found a prevalent issue, shift shock, which they describe as "that feeling when you start a new job and realize, with either surprise or regret, that the position or company is very different from what you were led to believe."[23] Seventy-two percent of respondents felt this shift shock, and 48 percent said they'd try to return to their old position if they experienced it. What's more, "80% said it's acceptable to leave a new job before six months if it doesn't live up to your expectations."[24]

And according to an CNBC article covering a Grant Thornton report, of the 21 percent of US workers who found a new job in the last year, "40% are already actively looking for another job."[25] Smart companies will learn how to ride the wave of this revolving door, especially since "so-called boomerangs accounted for 4.5% of all new hires among companies on LinkedIn in 2021, . . . up from 3.9% in 2019."[26]

The fact of the matter is, the world of work is always changing, and so is our relationship to talent and to work itself. But it can be hard to keep up.

Of course, chaos and uncertainty are fundamentally frightening. But after studying these shifts closely and working with leaders during these turbulent times, I've seen firsthand that the strongest leaders are the ones best able to look at the big picture and embrace agility. They look to the future instead of clinging to the past. They're willing to dig deep—personally and professionally. So, if you want to join the ranks of leaders whose companies are even stronger and more resilient than they were before 2020, you're going to have to let go of some of your most dearly held beliefs about business in general, and the employee life cycle in particular.

The time is now to reconsider everything we know about the employee journey and why linear thinking is being replaced by the more human reality of cycles, revolving doors, and dynamic change. As the management consultant firm Korn Ferry put it (about climate change, but it applies to the human organization too), "To become truly sustainable, organizations need to shift to a circular economy strategy."[27]

And please note that this time has come not just because of Covid and the social turmoil of 2020–2023, the combination of which has carried so many critical issues about power, identity, *real* authenticity, and mental health into mainstream conversations. Nor will any current or future round of unfortunate layoffs or other hits in the labor market affect the need for a new way of thinking about work. The fact is that even before these upheavals, the ways many leaders thought about the employee experience had not caught up to the tectonic shifts in our economy. Gone are the days of the IBMs and General Motors of the world offering employees a life of stability in exchange for commitment to the continued production of their wares. Today, we live in a service economy, held together by easy access to tech for both employees and consumers. This has given rise to gig workers who can move in and out of jobs as they see fit. Today, the power of flexible, remote, and asynchronous work is highlighted all the more, paving the way for those who are nimble and self-sufficient, and leaving behind those top leaders in golden handcuffs, confused and wondering when we'll be returning to the office, which is code for wondering when things will return to the way things *used to be.*

For the record, I don't think we're ever going back to the way things were. Nor should we.

Today, employees and companies join forces to create as much value as they can, together, moving in and out of connection in ways that actually benefit everyone involved—including shareholders. In fact, Great Place To Work found that treating employees well leads to higher stock prices. By a lot. In 2020, companies from their "Fortune 100 Best Companies to Work For" index outperformed the broader market by 16.5 percent.[28]

Instead of fixating on the price of turnover, shooting for stability at all costs, this book invites readers to consider how too much stability can lead to "languishing," to use Wharton professor and author Adam Grant's pandemic-famous word, or, good old-fashioned disengagement. According to Gallup's "State of the Global Workplace: 2022 Report," lack of engagement "cost the world $7.8 trillion in lost productivity . . . That's equal to 11% of global GDP."[29] Also according to Gallup, organizations in the top quartile for most-engaged employees are 23 percent *more profitable* than the bottom quartile.[30]

When it comes to cultivating a healthy pool of vibrant talent, the questions we should really be asking are: Who is leaving, and why? Are these people you can *afford* to lose?

Or are they going after a development opportunity you didn't provide? Or, maybe they don't feel like they belong, and it's time to take a long, hard look at your culture, and get those values off the walls and into the halls.

If all this out with the old, in with the new talk feels overwhelming or intimidating, rest assured you're in good company. Leaders and managers in every industry are anxious to know what they can do to transform their thinking and their teams to stay relevant and healthy in this new way of work. So, you're definitely not alone, and I'm honored to be your guide. Some of the work we'll do together is concrete, granular, and difficult. And some of it is incredibly simple, yet profound. Like with any paradigm shift, once you identify the places in your thinking that need to change, *voilà*, you're on your way.

CHAPTER ONE

START AS YOU MEAN TO GO ONBOARDING

OLD IDEA #1

Onboarding is that thing you do before the "real" work begins.

NEW BEGINNING #1

Onboarding sets the tone for what can hopefully be a long, possibly winding, but mutually beneficial relationship.

When my kids were little, I was obsessed with the British child psychologist Penelope Leach, whose mantra became my mantra: "Start as you mean to go on."

Which means, for example, if you want to raise a well-mannered young adult, you can begin by teaching your toddler how to clear their plate after a meal. Rinse, repeat a thousand times.

Onboarding anyone into anything—a family or a community or a company—is always a process of cocreation. We will always be creating some kind of culture, whether we're aware of it or not, by encouraging some behaviors and discouraging others. So, when we're the ones who get to set the tone, we have to be intentional right out of the gate.

Easier said than done, I know. Especially at work, when we have to fight against so many entrenched ways of doing business.

Remember when impersonal and transactional tasks like getting your parking spot, assigned seat, computer passwords, bathroom keys, and benefits packages passed for onboarding? When flipping through unreadable, corporate-speak handbooks was the stuff that would inspire a long-term, personal commitment to the company? Onboarding was the stuff that needed to happen before *real* work could begin. A box check.

Today at smart companies, onboarding is being rebranded, thankfully, as the beginning of that long and winding, mutually beneficial relationship. Onboarding is actually a way of welcoming someone for what Reid Hoffman, cofounder of LinkedIn, podcast host, and serial entrepreneur, calls a "tour of duty."[1] After all, in the Retention Revolution, employees are building their own careers as they pass through your company, coming and going—and perhaps, returning—all the while adding value, developing themselves and others, and sharing their wisdom.

These first interactions during the earliest days—even moments—of onboarding are an opportunity to share the tools employees will need to get the most out of the time we spend together—company values, the culture you're so proud of, and how each and every individual is so important. Yes, there's a lot of transactional work that must be done. But don't miss the boat! Paying attention to a person's need for purpose and community is the right thing—the *human* thing—to do, but it's also good for the bottom line. One of the most oft-repeated statistics you can find in pretty much every guide and article about onboarding is some version of, "Replacing an employee can cost up to two times their salary, so you better get this right!"[2]

Cut to today, where employees are honoring their relationships to themselves and their lives to such a degree that they are questioning whether or not they really want to keep a full-time job at all, let alone for the long haul. Yes, even—especially—in the midst of a cooling job market, when every penny spent on talent development counts.

One 2021 study of nearly 800 US employees who started new jobs during Covid found that "71% finished onboarding unsure of who they should 'build relationships with,' 62% didn't have a 'clear idea of the organization's culture,' and over half didn't have a clear idea of 'how to be productive in their role.' "[3] And a Glint study found that, "40 percent of employees who experienced a poor onboarding reported feeling disengaged three months later and would not recommend the company to others."[4]

A chief human resources officer at a large media company recently shared with me how they recruited a new person. No one even announced he was there for a full week. He felt invisible. Talk about starting as you *don't* mean to go on.

When it comes to onboarding new employees, the first step is to know where you're headed by having your values and culture goals firmly in place. Everything you do will arise out of that foundation. From there, you'll have to decide exactly what you need to cover to get someone up to speed. And then, you'll have to figure out how you're going to deliver all the info in a way that aligns with your values.

And it all starts, well, at the beginning.

The Three P's of Onboarding as You Mean to Go On

After studying the onboarding experiences of hundreds of companies over the years, I've discovered three simple ways to create a human onboarding experience that supports the Retention Revolution.

Make sure your onboarding is: Professional, Purposeful, and Personal. And yes, this goes for welcoming new employees whether you're in person, remote, in a cohort, one-on-one, or a mix of all the above.

Before March 2020, remote onboarding was hard to imagine—or may have seemed like an oxymoron. But for some, it's all they have known. Microsoft onboarded 60,000 new employees remotely from 2020 to 2022, which CEO Satya Nadella calls "the largest at-scale remote work experiment the world has seen."[5] And Microsoft's earnings have been no worse for the wear. Despite global turmoil from the war in Ukraine to pandemic-induced supply chain disruptions and chip shortages, revenue was up 12 percent for July's Q4 Fiscal Year 2022.[6]

I'll be sharing more about Nadella's grand experiment at the end of this chapter, but first, here's a great story about a pre-onboarding ritual.

But First . . . Onboarding Before the Onboarding

Gusto, a payroll, benefits, and HR platform, is ahead of the curve in culture and in business (as of May 2022 they were valued at almost $10 billion[7]), and in onboarding, as well.

Gusto has an amazing, deeply personal hiring ritual. Yep, that's pre-onboarding.

It starts when they put together a diverse, peer-nominated, carefully screened and trained interview team, which then conducts interviews with applicants with an eye for alignment in skill set, motivation, and values.

Which is pretty cool already. But here's the *really* cool part.

When Gusto decides to make an offer to a candidate, the hiring team (all the employees the potential new hire met as part of the interview process) hops on the offer call to cheer on and celebrate with them. After the cheering has died down, each team member from the hiring panel speaks about a moment from the candidate's interview that resonated with them, sharing why they are so excited to have the candidate potentially join the team.[8]

This pre-onboarding ritual stems from Gusto's early startup days, when there were just five people on the team and every employee interviewed the potential hire. According to CEO and cofounder Josh Reeves:

> *Since we were all working out of one room, when we did the offer call we didn't have any conference rooms to duck into. So we all joined in on the offer call. We would cheer and celebrate because we were really excited to find someone that was connected to our mission, values and philosophy. The cheering is a small thing, but it was authentic to us and we were genuinely really jazzed. And we've kept feeling this way with every offer, so we've kept doing it.*[9]

This kind of celebratory response would make any candidate feel welcome and excited to join. The fact that they're willing to invest the time and energy to start as they *might* go on shows just how much Gusto cares about the people they want on their team and how genuinely excited they are to have them. And even if a candidate decides not to join (which is unlikely, given Gusto's offer acceptance rate sits at a whopping 85 percent[10]), I bet they tell 10 of their friends how cool the hiring process was. And they tell their friends, and they tell their friends, and so on, and so on.

Take Onboarding Professionally

Some of the most important work we do is often very wrongly considered the easy part of the job, or the thing anyone could do if they just had the time. Think committee work, employee resource group (ERG) coordination, or event planning, to name a few. Traditionally, the onboarding process is part of HR's function, and farmed out to someone who has a hundred other things to do. But as I have often said, the soft stuff is the hard stuff. It deserves to be treated with respect, not as an add-on or an afterthought.

In other words, onboarding is an essential part of any business.

That's why the first step in onboarding well is to professionalize it. Depending on the size of your company, either hire someone whose sole job is to oversee onboarding or officially give it to someone in the organization to own and cultivate.

When you professionalize the onboarding process, the stakes are raised, and, hopefully, you'll be inspired to make it part of your company's culture and align it with your values. In other words, an intrinsic part of your work.

Because yes, onboarding should be fun, but it's also serious business.

Onboard Like a Unicorn with Stax

Stax is a payment merchant service founded in 2014 that reached "unicorn" status in March 2022.[11]

What exactly does that mean?

It means the company was valued at more than $1 billion. It also means that they know a thing or two about resilience during turbulent times.

At the beginning of 2020, Stax had 100 employees. Today, they have 335 and counting across four offices around the United States and Canada. Three of the offices are hybrid; the Orlando headquarters is "office first" but flexible. All of the offices are focused first and foremost on culture.

How can a company—how can *you*—not only manage, but grow and thrive during turbulent times?

By understanding that onboarding is serious business. So much so that you hire someone whose job it is to oversee it. Or, if you happen to have someone on staff who can and wants to do the job, by all means, let them own it—and of course, pay them for it.

Krystal Little, former Stax SVP business operations, shared with me how at the beginning of the pandemic, their sudden shift from being in person to remote actually helped her see how to grow their amazing culture—"what you would get if you were at the team lunch that day." So, they began by making sure that current team members had lots of time baked in for socializing and being "really, really intentional with our outreach to our teams . . . and then that brought us to our new hires."[12]

That intentionality—starting as they mean to go on—is what led them to hire a full-time professional dedicated to employee experience and onboarding. Enter a Stax employee who held a number of roles at the company for several years before being promoted to official manager of employee experience. Given the amount of talent growth Stax was experiencing, the manager's first job was to analyze, operationalize, and standardize the onboarding process. So, what does that look like?

When a cohort of new hires shows up to their first day at Stax, they're all met with the same three-hour introduction, led by a conversation about their culture. The manager talks about who Stax is, what their purpose is, and how they achieve that purpose through their core values, One Team, Create Joy, and Get It Done.

One of the manager's onboarding topics dives further into the first value—One Team—where they note, "We communicate with vulnerability and an open heart. We inspire each other as we work towards a common purpose and goal."[13] Orienting the very first meeting to their values shows new hires that, as the manager told me, "You don't just mean something to us from 9 to 5."[14]

It's no wonder Stax is crushing it. This is exactly the attitude employees today are looking for.

After inspiring excitement and feelings of connection, IT comes in to help the new employees get up and running. They receive their laptops, are given access to the system—the very nature of a payments platform necessitates extra tight security!—and a chance to get more familiar with it. A must-have for all, sure, but as Stax knows, *not* the place to start onboarding.

In the last hour before lunch, new hires learn about Stax life, and its impressive founding story. It's no accident that the first morning at Stax is bookended with content around culture and values.

Wisely, the manager's first morning structure also gives new hires a glimpse into how meetings are run in the broader organization. They get to see what a meeting is like at Stax—"collaborative, dynamic, ever-evolving, [and where] all ideas are welcome"[15]—which helps prepare them for meetings down the road.

If you read my book *Rituals Roadmap*, you know how important onboarding rituals are, which is why I was so happy to learn that the cohort's last—but definitely not least—to-do on day one is the group photo. The onboarding photo captures and memorializes the moment, cementing this group of new hires.

I asked the manager if the new hire cohorts bond and stay connected post-onboarding. They shared that they recently ran into two employees from the same onboarding group who were planning to have lunch together. The employee described her cohort lunch date as her "day one girl!" By the way, if you haven't heard the famous Gallup best friend at work stat, here goes: "Employees who have a best friend at work are significantly more likely to: engage customers and internal partners, get more done in less time, support a safe workplace with fewer accidents and reliability concerns, innovate and share ideas, [and] have fun while at work."[16] And since the pandemic, there's been an even stronger correlation between business outcomes and having a best friend at work.[17]

The second day of onboarding is a little more relaxed, but no less intentional. New hires spend the first 30 minutes with their department to get familiarized with their teammates. Then, they spend the day going over shared units: marketing, security and compliance, risk and underwriting, and so on. By breaking this flood of new information, new systems, and new people into two days, the manager gives the new hires a chance to soak everything in and better acclimate.

And as you can see, none of it is left up to chance. Every piece of the onboarding process is intentional, establishes the company's vision, and sets up the new employees for success.

So, what are the business implications of this very professional two-day onboarding process? Little reports that their onboarding has led to a reduction in turnover.

MURAL

Accenture, a global professional services firm, uses the digital whiteboard tool, Mural, to make human connections with new hires during the onboarding process.

Luke Brodie, client innovation services lead at Accenture's Canada Innovation Hub, showed me the virtual board game his team created for new employees to complete using Mural in their first 48 hours on the job. The game has practical tasks, such as watching welcome videos, completing compliance training, booking one-on-ones with people managers, and getting set up in team chats, which is a great sweet spot start. But it also includes fun "get to know you" prompts, like, "Rank your top 3 pizza toppings" and "What song is the soundtrack to your life?" along with physical breaks, like, "Put a 1 minute timer on and do desk stretches" and "Go outside for 5 minutes and get some sun."[18]

There's real thought behind the game—it's designed to show new hires how to prioritize and practice the skills they will use on the job every day, from getting comfortable with tech tools (such as Mural itself) to leadership skills such as storytelling, "so that they can be successful later." And, Brodie notes, "We've been able to shorten onboarding time and increase a sense of connection to our team."[19]

Accenture's use of Mural hits every onboarding mark—Brodie is the professional who owns the process, it's connected to Accenture's purpose ("To deliver on the promise of technology and human ingenuity"), and by weaving "get to know you" questions throughout, they've made it personal.

Onboarding on Purpose

A recent study by McKinsey & Company found that "70 percent of employees said that their sense of purpose is defined by their work."[20] It just so happens that the best companies are also purpose-driven. So much so that employees are willing to make real sacrifices to work at purpose-driven organizations. A survey from LinkedIn found that "86% of young employees reported being willing to give ground on title and compensation to work at a business aligned with their values or mission."[21]

Onboarding is the perfect time to create that important meeting of the minds and make the connection between a new hire's roles and the purpose of the organization.

Nice to Meet You, Says Meetup

Meetup is a platform that helps people make connections with like-minded folks for, well, a meetup. Up until 2020, these Meetups were in-person gatherings, but during the pandemic they added virtual meetings to keep its members connected. Today, members have the option to host virtual Meetups, but the company places a strong emphasis on the value of meeting in real life (otherwise known as IRL).

Meetup CEO David Siegel has made sure that employee hiring and onboarding is aligned with their core value and business proposition of making quality connections. Specifically, Siegel shared with me that no matter what their job responsibility, everything they do connects to the company's mission to help drive community and connections between people. Which is why, "As soon as someone accepts [the offer of employment]," Siegel explained, "I send them a personal email, welcoming them to the company. In it, I specifically map their role to how it connects to the larger mission of Meetup."[22]

Here are a couple of real examples that Siegel has sent:

I was so excited to hear the great news that you will be joining Meetup. Have heard such great feedback from E., H. and others about you. Program management and ensuring great operations will elevate all our product team efforts and drive meaningful impact. Such a critical role.

See you in August . . . and take care,

David

I've heard such great feedback about you from ML, Harry and others. Your role in customer success at Pro is insanely important to Meetup. Pro is the fastest growing area at Meetup, and building and growing relationships with our clients is incredibly critical. Can't wait until your 8/15 start and enjoy the weekend! Especially in San Diego . . .

Best,

David

A welcome from the CEO may not sound like much, but it's an incredibly effective and impactful way to put a pin in shared purpose. It's not uncommon for new employees to receive a welcome package, but as Siegel says, "people know that everyone gets the same package."[23] A generic swag bag doesn't necessarily tie a person to the company's purpose and—worst-case scenario—can even contribute to a feeling of disconnection.

As you can see, onboarding at Meetup is more than just an introduction. It's a perfectly poised moment to infuse the company's ultimate purpose into people's minds.

Not surprisingly, "Inevitably every person returns my email saying, wow, I can't believe that the CEO took the time to send me a personal welcome."[24] They can't believe the CEO took time to say, "Nice to meet you."

Twilio's Scarlet Jacket

It's your first day of work in marketing at Twilio, the tech company that makes it possible for your Uber driver to tell you that you've arrived or for the restaurant host to alert you when your table's ready. You're put in a group with a bunch of developers and taught how to make an app.

Next you have to demo it . . . live . . . in front of a bunch of colleagues.

And then, you receive your very own red track jacket. You've joined the Twilio club, and boy have you earned it.

The scarlet track jacket is an important part of the Twilio onboarding process. It links each person—regardless of their role—to the company's purpose, which is to create customer engagement using technology. Of course, the company needs all manner of experts to shine, but at its heart it's a tech company; this onboarding ritual helps everyone get a taste of what that means.

As Christy Lake, chief people officer at Twilio shared with me, "It goes back to the ethos of who we are. Our founder and CEO felt like everybody at the company should be a developer."[25] From Lake's perspective, this onboarding ritual is a two for one: It helps orient new hires as to, "this is what we do, this is how a developer interacts with us," and it's also a visual symbol that "I'm a developer too, I'm part of this company. I'm part of the culture."

"I'm a part of this company's purpose."

You might be wondering if this important ritual is still a thing for remote and hybrid workers. The answer is yes. As Lake told me, it was a little tricky in the early days of virtual onboarding, but it's back.[26] In fact, Lake rocks her very own track jacket from time to time over Zoom—not by chance, but on purpose.

Generational Onboarding at Rowland+Broughton

Rowland+Broughton (R+B) is an architecture design firm located in Aspen, Colorado. Principal Sarah Broughton was at a conference when she heard a presentation on understanding generational insights. Thinking about the challenges of running a firm of 44 people across Gen X, millennials, and Gen Z—with many baby boomer clients—a light bulb went off! Broughton shared with me, "What if we learned about generational differences and introduced it to our employees? If employees understand who [they] are working with and for—and their generational tendencies, it sets everyone up for success!"[27] Broughton decided to make onboarding more purposeful by incorporating generational insights from day one.

Here is how it works: new hires at Rowland+Broughton have a multiday onboarding with checkpoints at 30, 60, and 90 days. They are assigned someone from the R+B onboarding committee, who is trained to be very deliberate about onboarding.

They also spend time with the director of human resources, who takes new hires through a presentation called "Decoding Demographic Shifts and Understanding Generational Insights for Success." The presentation provides an overview of each generation's core values, work ethic, communication practices, feedback preferences, and stereotypes.

New hires receive lots of examples for how to succeed in a multi-generational environment. For example, "If you have a meeting with a Gen X team member, here are some tools for success. Know that the Gen Xer will poke lots of holes in your ideas. She comes at the issues through the Generation X lens. It is who she is."

The generational onboarding presentation also shares some important reminders:

- Everyone has to bend a little and see things through the lens of others. Talk to your team about your style of communication.
- Understand the priorities and styles of each team member to create powerful project delivery and career trajectory.
- Avoid the "you don't get to have what I have unless you go through it exactly as I did" mentality.

Broughton went on to share, "This is about creating understanding. Not about highlighting bad behavior. Having this type of information helps employees collaborate with a diverse group of people and create project success."[28]

Wow, I wish I'd had this during the onboarding in my past jobs!

Make It Personal

Imagine two scenarios where you're attending a conference. In the first scenario, you're greeted with a badge and a quick hello, leaving you on your own to find your way to the presentations you'll enjoy.

In the second scenario, a host is assigned to kindly introduce you to someone they think you'll like, who introduces you to someone else and so on.

Which conference would you rather go to?

Me? I'm headed to number two.

Think of onboarding in the same way. Personal connections are curated and never left up to chance. Because, as I always say, left to our own devices, we're not connecting.

In other words, make onboarding personal.

One of my favorite superhuman CEOs, Satya Nadella of Microsoft, joined Adam Grant on his podcast, *Re:Thinking*, where he shared a best practice from one of his senior leaders, who found a way to be intentional when introducing new employees to his team. Nadella recalls, "He took real care in introducing the person who came into Microsoft to all the people personally, like he would in fact, set up the [Microsoft] Teams call and make the introduction and then leave the Teams call so that then she could actually have the one-on-one with the person."[29] Even at a company built and centered around technology, with a virtual meeting made possible by technology, the simple, human factor—a personal introduction—was still the most important touch in making a new hire feel welcome.

Making onboarding personal isn't rocket science, but that doesn't make it easy. As you're thinking about onboarding, think about the conference that you would rather go to or the company you would rather work for.

For me, it's a pretty easy decision. The one that makes us feel connected to others from the beginning is the place we all want to be.

The Humu-n Touch
(Or Nudge as the Case May Be)

Finally, one of the most impressive, human companies I've come across is Humu, a software platform founded in 2017 by former Google executives. Humu uses carefully crafted, research-backed digital "nudges" to help leaders and teams improve and get results.

They're masters in finding the sweet spot between tech and connect (more on that later), but what's even more impressive is how they walk the walk with their own teams, onboarding their new hires—better known as "Numus"— with a very personal touch.

Because their onboarding is so impressive, I'm going to get into some step-by-step detail, shared with me by Daniel Huerta, former demand generation manager and the CEO and cohost of the *Modern People Leader* podcast.

Before Day One: Numus complete a "get to know you" questionnaire and receive both a detailed roadmap of the first two weeks on the job and an email from their manager, complimenting them on all the great things they noticed during the interview process. They're also introduced to their Numu Buddy.

As Huerta explained to me, "They want [the Numu Buddy] to be somebody that's cross functional, somebody that they know that you're going to work with a lot."[30] He goes on to recall his Buddy's intro:

> *Hey, so excited to have you on the team. I just want to introduce myself. I'm Dina. I'm going to be your Numu Buddy. If you have any questions about anything, let me know. I'm also going to be the one that intros you to the broader Humu team. And I'm going to be here to guide you the first couple of weeks, if you have any questions.*[31]

Definitely more comforting than "Here's your laptop," I'd say.

On Day One: Intending to replicate the in-office experience, where employees once stood around a new employee's "balloon-strewn desk,"[32] Numus are now greeted with a virtual, companywide meet and greet on their first day. The call starts with a prompt like, "What was your favorite childhood movie?" And then the new and current employees get to share. After, they have a Numu Buddy hang, before hopping on various calls about culture and strategy and having a one-on-one with their manager.

Over the Next Two Weeks: During this time, various "get to know you" meetings are scheduled, but none more exciting and inspirational than the chat with Laszlo Bock, cofounder and then-CEO (now board chair) of Humu. It's understandable that new hires would feel nervous in their first meeting with the CEO. But in true Humu fashion, they can be expected to be treated with empathy.

As Huerta recalls from his own onboarding, Bock said:

> *All we expect from you is to soak in as much information as you can, meet as many people as you can, don't feel like you need to prove anything. You've already proven your worth and that you belong to be here. You belong. You belong here at the company.*[33]

I love this! Any way you slice it, the first few days, weeks, months of a new job are stressful. Bock and Humu are giving their new hires permission to get to know their new job and new colleagues in whatever way works for them—without anything to prove.

Day Fourteen: Humu onboarding officially ends two weeks later, with a Numu graduation ceremony. In preparation for graduation, the hiring managers reach out to the Numu's teammates to hear about what they have accomplished over those two weeks. Then, those accomplishments are recounted and celebrated in front of the whole company.

Imagine!

But wait, there's more (if you can believe it). As Huerta told me:

> *You also receive an email where they've gathered quotes from the 10 people that you interacted with the most, where they all say a bunch of really nice*

things about you. So you open your email at like
nine in the morning. It's the first email you see, it's
like, "Happy Graduation, Daniel!" You open it and
you get to read all of the nice things that all of your
coworkers have to say about you.[34]

Wow!

And Finally: After the Numu graduation, the head of IT puts together a video with a montage of clips from the ceremony, including every manager's speech. This launches their "Smile File"—I kid you not—a directory of positive emails, texts, videos, and more, from friends, colleagues, or their boss that they can reference whenever they're "having a bad day or when [they] receive a particularly critical piece of feedback."[35]

Yes, even people with Smile Files have to give and receive hard feedback.

Next, colleagues are invited (with a nudge of course!) to add positive feedback to the Numu's Smile File, which "helps set the tone for Humu's culture of genuine appreciation and gratitude. When people feel that their efforts are recognized, they're more likely to continue doing great work."[36]

And great work begets more great work.

This is onboarding as you mean to go on, and on.

PS: And That's Not All: Full-Circle Re-onboarding with Microsoft

OK, back to Satya Nadella's "grand experiment," onboarding 60,000 people remotely in 2020 (which we discussed at the beginning of this chapter). Remember how he was willing to invest so much time and money into that process because he understands that in the Retention Revolution, "[Employees] are one of the most important stakeholders. Without employees, there is no company"?[37]

Well, that's not all.

He also knows that when we're facing massive shifts in the way we work and live, like we all are today, it's not just new hires who need to be welcomed aboard, but "the entirety of the company needs to be re-onboarded."[38]

And that's exactly what they're doing.

I had the pleasure of speaking with Joe Whittinghill, Microsoft's corporate VP of talent, learning, and insights, about how the entire company (more than 200,000 people) is currently going through a process of "re-onboarding and onboarding to our culture," by asking everyone to participate in what they're calling a "three-hour culture conversation."[39]

Inspired by the turmoil of 2020, Whittinghill started having what he called "Values Conversations" as his "solution to how we deal with some of the stuff that was happening in society. I said we need to have a values conversation. The amazing result . . . was off the charts."[40]

So, when it became clear that onboarding was something the entire company could use as they found their way out of the pandemic, he piggybacked on what was working and decided to launch the "Culture Conversation."

According to one of his senior leaders at Microsoft, "I didn't think this was going to be that big of a deal . . . but my team is so fired up because one of the questions we ask is, What keeps you at Microsoft?"[41]

So, what exactly is a culture conversation, and how can you incorporate this idea into your team as a means of re-onboarding?

These conversations are a three-hour dialogue between a senior leader and their organization, held in groups of 50 or fewer. Leaders receive a facilitator's guide, designed by a Microsoft employee with a background in education, so everyone is on the same page.

The key to the culture conversation's success is that it's led by senior leaders, not by HR. This is so important because it pushes managers to tell personal stories, to facilitate, and to guide, which is also great professional development for them.

According to Whittinghill, there will be more than 4,000 culture conversations that happen over the course of a year, and that Microsoft CEO Nadella already had his conversation with his direct reports.

At Microsoft's scale, this is a pretty overwhelming proposition, but for many companies, it's just a very well-crafted and consistent conversation that brings the entire community to a shared sense of purpose. "And if you do that, the outcome is belonging."[42]

Isn't that the truth?!

He continues:

If people don't feel they belong, they're going to vote with their feet and go somewhere that they can belong. And with the labor market, it's going to be that way for the foreseeable future. We want everyone to feel that they belong. And then let's be honest, the offboarding piece is, and after two years they may decide, hey, this isn't really my jam, and so I'm going to go try some other place and we're good with that, but then we want to have a respectful offboarding process.[43]

And that, my friends, is the virtuous cycle of the Retention Revolution.

That's a (W)RAP

Retention Action Plan for Onboarding

1. Assess the onboarding program at your organization. What happens on the first day of work (or even before the first day of work, as soon as the offer is made)? When possible, onboard new hires as a cohort. This gives your new hires an instant community and a built-in support group.

2. Align your onboarding program with your company's values. This is a great way to bring your values to life from day one. For example, if collaboration is an important value, show how you collaborate during the onboarding process.

3. Consider who should be involved in the onboarding process. Human resources? The hiring manager? A buddy? All of them? Onboarding is a team sport and, ideally, many different people are involved in helping your new hires get up and running. The more touch points the better!

4. Design a lot of touch points (see Number Three above) at regular intervals, e.g., at the end of the first week, month, quarter, etc. A successful onboarding program goes well beyond the first day. Plan a reunion for the new-hire cohort. Make it a ritual.

5. Feedback, feedback, feedback! Ask your new hires how you can improve and evolve the program. Consider involving your new hires in the onboarding process for the next group of new hires.

CHAPTER TWO

SAY GOODBYE TO THE LIFESTYLES OF THE RICH AND FLEXIBLE AND HELLO TO FLEX FOR ALL

OLD IDEA #2

Employees are only working when you can see them.

NEW BEGINNING #2

It's official. Autonomy and flexibility are good for business, great for people, and just might change the world.

"I'll call in from the Hamptons."

Never has a phrase suggested success quite like this one.

Before 2020, that is.

Back in the day, having the privilege to call in implied you were probably floating on a yacht somewhere, peeling yourself away from your fabulous friends to take this *very important* call.

Calling in was part of the lifestyle of the rich and flexible.

And that's because before 2020, flexibility, like most benefits and perks, was something you earned over time—an incentive for hanging in there and climbing to the tippy top of the corporate ladder.

Today, not only is remote or hybrid work often the norm for many people, but as a 2022 *Wall Street Journal* article pointed out, in some cases, it's now the bosses who are the ones stuck in the office, trying to entice their teams back in.[1]

The reality is, the genie is out of the bottle on this one; too many people have tasted the perks of working from anywhere, and they're just not buying it. Nor should they. Georgetown professor Nick Lovegrove points out,

"Companies need to ask themselves why there's been this de facto rebellion against the office, and that's because it kind of sucked."[2] So much so that in a September 2022 Monster Work Watch Report, 26 percent of survey respondents said they'd "rather get a root canal—the notoriously painful dental procedure—than work in their offices five days a week."[3] Dramatic? Yes. Telling? No doubt.

According to a 2022 McKinsey report, 58 percent of Americans have the opportunity to work from home at least one day a week, and 35 percent report having the option to work from home five days a week.[4] That's a lot of flexibility out there in the market right now. But in some parts of the world, postpandemic flexibility does not seem to be as big of a focus. According to a March 2023 CNBC article, "office attendance has returned to 70% to 90% in Europe and the Middle East, and around 80% to 110% in some Asian cities, meaning some workers are spending more time in the office now than pre-Covid."[5] Though these data are always a moving target, it's best to simply expect that flexibility in some form will always be important, especially to new generations.

Now, one might assume these US percentages refer only to people with desk jobs, but, as the McKinsey report notes, "What makes these numbers particularly notable is that respondents work in all kinds of jobs, in every part of the country and sector of the economy, including traditionally labeled 'blue collar' jobs that might be expected to demand on-site labor."[6]

Which is why we need to take a step back and try to see the bigger picture. Success in the Retention Revolution requires less reactivity and more strategy. Less control and more trust. Less obsessing over hours logged and more focusing on results and outcomes. Less loyalty points for perks, and more start as you mean to go on.

The idea of flexible work—and all that it entails and implies—is at the forefront of so many discussions about the future of work because it affects our everyday lives so deeply. For employees, the stakes are high and very personal: commute or no commute; hiring someone to pick up the kids or walk the dog, or doing it ourselves; grabbing lunch with friends and colleagues, or eating alone with your camera off during yet another virtual meeting; being seen and appreciated (and promoted?) or being productive in the peace and quiet of home; bracing for the impact of microaggressions from well-meaning (or not) coworkers, or feeling safe.

For employers, the stakes are also very high: decisions around real estate holdings, uncertainty about productivity means and measures, massive talent upheaval, scary headlines to decipher, managing new managers, recession, inflation, and volatility.

Indeed, the topic of this chapter—flexibility and autonomy—is a life-changing revolution in and of itself, but it's not particularly new. In my 2018 book, *Bring Your Human to Work*, I referred to the 2014 survey by the Global Leadership Summit in London, where 34 percent of business leaders said that "more than half their company's full-time workforce would be working remotely by 2020."[7]

Which is to say, this is not a new phenomenon, but one that has gathered so much steam, there's no going back.

As reported in a 2022 *Fast Company* article by Karen Kaplan, chair and CEO of Hill Holliday, a Boston-based communications agency, "The pandemic gave people a greater appreciation for flexibility—whether that looks like remote work options [or] an asynchronous work schedule,"[8] which we can all agree on. But did you know that "when employees are satisfied with their company's flexible accommodations they are 2.6 times more likely to be happy and 2.1 times more likely to recommend working for the company"?[9]

A Future Forum survey of more than 10,000 knowledge workers across six continents found that 76 percent want flexibility in where they work and a whopping 93 percent of workers said they want flexibility in *when* they work.[10]

A McKinsey study of more than 25,000 people found that when people have the chance to work flexibly, 87 percent of them take it.[11] And again, this is true for all kinds of workers—across demographic, age, types of jobs, etc.—and even more so for people of color and marginalized groups. In fact, in the study, employees with disabilities were 11 percent more likely and LBGTQ+ employees were 13 percent more likely to prefer hybrid work.[12]

There's absolutely no doubt that, as Kaplan puts it, "flexibility is a competitive advantage."[13]

So, where do we start?

In researching this book, it's been my job (lucky me!) to interview forward-thinking leaders, read books and articles, and listen to podcasts about this new world of work. When it comes to the huge and thorny issue of flexibility, there's so much to explore; I've found a big part of the discussion is about how to start organizing the conversation in a productive and meaningful way.

"It's not the where, it's the *who*," some say, referring to the way remote work has invited so many nontraditional and global workers into the mix.

"It's not the where, it's the *what*," according to others, looking at how we can unravel workstreams to make more sense for flexible work.

"It's not the what, it's the *how*," is yet another approach, playing a game of scheduling Tetris, trying to find the perfect mix of in-person and remote work.

To me the answer is: all of the above.

As you'll see, the best way to make work really work for all, is to be flexible about flexibility.

How to ACE Flexibility for All

In 2018, TIAA, a financial services organization with more than 15,000 employees, took a hard line. Some of their teams were remote, though not part of a formal program, and the top execs had had enough. They decided they wanted everyone in (or near) an office. In addition to wanting to be sure people were available for in-person collaboration and connection, the bifurcated model of some in the office and some out of the office created a lack of cohesion within the culture. However, the announcement didn't go well, especially since many employees would have to move to meet the mandate. So, instead, while some made the move, many others were disgruntled, took a severance package, and left.

What a difference a few years makes.

Sean N. Woodroffe, TIAA's senior executive vice president and chief people officer at the time, talked to me about how, as of 2022, they've rolled out what they call "radical flexibility."[14] Today, TIAA offers employees three options right out of the hiring gate: remote flex, hybrid flex, and office flex. Employees can choose their primary orientation based on position, but there's always some flex available. This does make it pretty radical, especially since flexibility isn't earned, but assumed.

Even for companies like TIAA that are ready to offer flexibility to all employees from the beginning, there is still much to understand about implementation. Putting a flex stake in the ground is your first step. Ongoing iteration on how it will work in your company is the next.

So, next I'll break it down and show you how to ACE flexibility by offering people what we know they want: Autonomy, Connection, and Equity.

Autonomy: Productivity Paranoia Will Destroy You

It's only human to want to check in with your employees. Even the most respectful managers and leaders in the world are subtly checking in, taking note of comings and goings, developing an appreciation for their individual workers. It's your job, in fact, to observe and assess your team's performance.

Which is why I understand that it can feel difficult to trust that employees are working when you can't see them.

And yet, the time has come. As Eve Rodsky, author of *Fair Play*, put it, "I've heard many leaders conflate working from home with flexible work. Choosing where you work is not the same thing as flexibility over how you work, and when you work."[15]

And it's that kind of flexibility—or autonomy—that means everything to employees today.

And as Phil Kirschner of McKinsey points out, "The desire for autonomy transcends income levels, ages, demographics. Everyone wants a good amount of it."[16] And while clearly autonomy is more accessible for knowledge workers, the call for it can be heard from frontline workers as well, which I'll discuss later in this chapter. As Professors Rebecca Johannsen and Paul J. Zak noted in their original research paper, "Autonomy Raises Productivity: An Experiment Measuring Neurophysiology," published in May 2020, empowering employees "increase[s] productivity . . . resulting in improved mood."[17]

And finally, because more and more companies are figuring out how to offer autonomy, it's in your company's best interest to do the same if you want to stay competitive.

But how do you offer autonomy when we're so conditioned to feel like we have to watch over people?

One option taken by some companies is to go all-out and track employees' every move of the mouse for productivity scores, which has inspired a new line of products developed by said employees to keep their mouse in motion.[18]

If there was ever a crossed wire of opportunity, this is it! I mean, wouldn't you rather these brilliant folks channel their creativity into your company, rather than side hustling to fool your system?

Microsoft's research on the state of hybrid work in 2022 pointed to the issue of productivity paranoia as a major hurdle for managers.[19] So much so that *Vox* writer Rani Molla called out productivity theater as the latest major time and attention drain for many workers who "frequently update their status on Slack . . . they say hello and goodbye, and they drop into different channels throughout the day to chitchat. They check in with managers and just tell anyone what they're working on. They even join meetings they don't need to be in (and there are many more meetings) and answer emails late into the night."[20]

This behavior is bad for business. As Nancy Baym, senior principal research manager at Microsoft, points out, "When people trust one another . . . you get a willingness to take risks, you get more innovation and creativity and less group-think."[21] Which is our goal, right?

Definitely. But trust isn't exactly a silver bullet, either.

Sid Sijbrandij, cofounder and CEO of GitLab, the biggest all-remote company in the world with 1,200 team members in 65 countries says:

> *Of course, we assume that people have good intentions, but managers are here to make sure that the results get delivered and that the results get measured. If you work in sales, we measure how much you sell and how happy the customers are. If you work in support, it's how fast do we respond to customers? If you work in engineering, how fast were you able to ship things?*[22]

In other words, when productivity is understood as time spent instead of results delivered, you miss the point entirely. Sijbrandij continues, "You will get what you measure."

This bears repeating. It's not that we just want to measure what matters; it works the other way around. What we measure *becomes* what we create.

He goes on, "So if you measure key strokes, you'll get key strokes. If you measure hours, you'll get hours. So it's a big mistake to measure both of these, because they don't push your business forward. It's so much more important to measure results,"[23] especially when it comes to autonomy.

Colette Stallbaumer, general manager at Microsoft 365 and Future of Work Marketing, agrees:

> *It's misplaced energy to focus on whether people are working enough. Leaders need to create clarity*

*on what to prioritize. It sounds simple but the data
shows it's harder than we think. Empower people
and help them understand what's most important.
Your people will thank you for it.*[24]

In the Retention Revolution, deciding what to measure, then communicating it clearly is absolutely critical in any work environment. And by the way, I've never met a company that overcommunicates, so don't hesitate to tell people what's on your mind! What matters is that we bring increased autonomy to our employees, wherever they are.

What follows are just a few of the many ways you can start shifting your mindset to create autonomy for your teams. It's important to start small, but don't stop there. As writer and entrepreneur Steve Glaveski writes in the *Harvard Business Review*, "Well-meaning band-aid solutions achieve little if the toxic norms that rob knowledge workers of autonomy and control remain in place."[25]

Wow, and Then Some: Creating Autonomy for All Teams

In early 2020, Neiman Marcus Group (NMG), led by Eric Severson, chief people and belonging officer, launched the NMG Way of Working (WOW) model.

And it really is a *wow*.

As he told me, "We empower our associates to work whenever, however, and wherever to best achieve results. This is about productivity, effective decision-making, transparency, and empowerment—attributes that create both a high-performing and highly engaged workforce."[26]

To further ensure this new way of working *works*, Severson also rolled out companywide commitments, which help both desk and deskless—like retail and distribution—associates have autonomy over some aspects of their work.

Corporate teams, for instance, have core meeting hours (Monday to Thursday, 9 a.m. to 5 p.m. [CST]), focus Fridays (after 1 p.m. [CST]), and corporate recharge weeks (not a week *off*, but fewer meetings with minimal distractions and personal time off [PTO] encouraged), and they make well-being a central driver of the program.

And in the stores, NMG's retail associates enjoy generous flexibility, choosing both *where* they will work (which store and department) and *when* they will work (what days and hours). Neiman Marcus's innovative customer app also provides empowering possibilities for associates to continue their customer relationships off the sales floor (e.g., earning commission through links posted on social media, sent via text, or through the NMG app's own messaging function), inspiring an entrepreneurial spirit and focus on long-term relationship building.

These commitments are intended to provide guardrails for employees that are ultimately tied to accountability and trust to get the job done in a way that works for both employees and NMG.

And here's a really cool—and very important—part of rolling out something so new and innovative. Severson and his team laid out, not only what WOW *is*, but also, what it is *not*, such as:

- A reason to avoid a corporate hub if it is essential to achieve results
- A license to be unavailable or unaccountable

- An end to planning and structure (NMG|WOW requires *more* planning, in some cases)

Severson summed it up this way: "NMG|WOW is built to accommodate associates' professional and personal commitments in a way that prioritizes the health and well-being of their families and themselves."[27]

Autonomy can also be built into the workday, like at shaving company Harry's, where they instituted the concept of "golden time," or GT. The company instituted calendar blocks as part of their return-to-office plan—again, the majority of employees are now hybrid. Employees are expected to block off a certain amount of time on their calendar; no one is allowed to book over it. This gives people the opportunity to choose how they spend their day. People can use the block to exercise, take care of appointments, or just take a break. According to Katie Childers, chief people officer at Harry's, the hope of this initiative is to give employees "a feeling of empowerment to take what they need from a flexibility perspective."[28]

Autonomy isn't just about when and where we work; it's also about having time off that is predictable so that we can work our lives around it.

One well-known study by Leslie A. Perlow and Jessica L. Porter (which ultimately became the 2012 book *Sleeping with Your Smartphone*) tracked consultants from Boston Consulting Group (BCG), some of the most round-the-clock workers. If you think this was a long time ago, you're right! So much has changed, and yet the culture of BCG at the time might sound familiar: "When people are 'always on,' responsiveness becomes ingrained in the way they work, expected by clients and partners, and even institutionalized in performance metrics."[29]

At the end of four years of research, Perlow and Porter found that "consultants and other professionals can provide the highest standards of service and still have planned, uninterrupted time off."[30] A.k.a. autonomy. If you still think today's market makes this too difficult, consider this: "They can do this even in times of recession."[31]

While some employees benefit from the autonomy of predictable time off, others are in desperate need of predictable time *on*. In other words, for frontline, hourly, deskless workers, autonomy is even more important because they're so often called into work at a moment's notice and—at the same time—stuck with shifts that don't work for their life commitments. Which is why companies like Starbucks, Amazon.com, and Walmart are all experimenting with policies and apps that give workers more scheduling flexibility. Likewise, some call centers are letting people work from home.[32]

Some employers have moved away from the typical nine-to-five, Monday through Friday schedule to offer more flexibility in terms of the number of days worked and shift length. Of course, this depends on each organization's business and customer needs, but the key is to give more autonomy and agency to employees over how and when they're scheduled. Using a shift marketplace allows colleagues to swap, offer, or pick up shifts without any need for management involvement. An employer could even give employees the chance to self-schedule. One large retailer who adopted this approach saw an increase in employee engagement and a decrease in last-minute callouts.[33]

General Mills is an organization with more than 30,000 employees, 18,000 of whom are deskless, working across 46 plants. According to General Mills CHRO Jacqueline

Williams-Roll, "Flexibility at General Mills is table stakes. Everyone deserves flexibility regardless of where you work."[34]

Yep, even in a manufacturing plant.

According to Renee Lash, senior human resources director of their North American manufacturing and supply chain, the flexibility framework within the plants is in place to help teams "see the breadth of opportunities that exist as we think about employee choice, autonomy, and flexibility." Things they keep in mind include:

- **When I work.** This includes providing employees with autonomy over shift swaps (e.g., finding a teammate to cover an overtime block or posting for additional hours), programs focused on leveraging retirees to work select hours or shifts or cover a leave, and exploring alternative schedules based on employee feedback and choice (including traditional 8-hour shifts, 12-hour shifts, or part-time schedules).
- **Where I work.** By utilizing bid processes and empowered work team systems, employees have input into *where* within the operation they want to work, allowing them to leverage their skills and capabilities.
- **What I work on.** Employees should be encouraged to opt in to learning and development opportunities and cross-training to grow their skills and progress their career, select individual roles or job responsibilities across their team, recommend improvement opportunities, and lead or participate in those efforts.
- **Whom I work with.** In addition to employee choice in the jobs that they bid for, provide opportunities for employees to join various committees and improvement teams.

- **How I work.** Allow employees opportunities to define ways of working, team norms, and rituals by participating in daily direction-setting meetings to develop the plan for the day for their system or line. Engage in regular focus group discussions with local leadership to share ideas, needs, and perspectives on how to make the work and our operations better.

As Deborah Lovich from BCG puts it, "The world saw the importance of deskless workers during the pandemic. They allowed the rest of us to remain productive while working remotely. Today, they watch after our children and our elderly; they build our bridges and operate the trucks and trains that deliver the goods we require for work and life. If they flee their jobs, we will all pay the price."[35]

Which is exactly why the Retention Revolution is all about the virtuous cycle. We're all in this together. When autonomy is available to all, everyone wins.

THE **SWEET SPOT** BETWEEN **TECH & CONNECT**

SCOOP

Many employees actually do want to go to the office, but only if they are there intentionally, with the right colleagues. Nobody wants to show up to an empty office to be on video calls all day.

Enter Scoop, the company committed to making flexible work effortless and universal. Their motto?

"Office Days should feel like awesome days!" Who would disagree with that?

So, what is Scoop?

Scoop is a scheduling assistant app that integrates with Slack, calendars, and Chrome. Employees can mark and update where they'll be working—from home, from the office, or out of office altogether—using an emoji. Scoop also offers polls to organize group schedules and automates invites to coworkers for in-person coffees and lunches. By simplifying coordination, employees can better plan their hybrid workweeks, maximizing time for collaboration and in-person connection.

And with the enterprise version of Scoop, employers can access HR integration, data, and insights, which help them determine which teams go into the office when, meeting planning, proximity bias, turnover correlation, exec team versus direct reports attendance, and office sizing needs.

What's the result? As CEO and cofounder Rob Sadow told me, several companies using Scoop have seen office attendance double because employees finally had visibility on who was going to the office.[36]

One of Scoop's clients, Kivvit, has even turned Scoop into a verb. Molly Scherrman, Kivvit COO, told me they'll ask each other, "Did you Scoop today?" Before using Scoop, they didn't have a way to track office fluctuations, but now they can boost participation and efficiency, and they make informed decisions based on the data from Scoop. Oh, and fun fact: according to their Scoop data, Friday is the least popular day in the office—as you might've guessed.

PS: Scoop recently introduced their Flex Index, crowdsourcing hybrid/office/remote policies from approximately 4,000 companies (and counting!). Similar to Glassdoor's review of company culture, this tool aims to give prospective hires a more accurate picture of what an organization's hybrid policy looks like in practice.[37]

Connection: When We're Left to Our Own Devices

The way technology impacts our relationships has been a central theme in public discourse for decades. And the stakes are even higher with the steep rise in use of devices during the pandemic—even with tools designed for connection, like video chat and Slack. We're connecting, sure, but are we *really*?

Maybe these days it's more like this: left to our own devices, we're not connecting as well as we could . . . whether virtually or in person, even in the office.

Sean N. Woodroffe from TIAA described the dilemma: "Why do we have to come in? We worked well, we were productive [working from home]. And my response to that is, well, at what cost? The notion that we can be away from each other indefinitely . . . it has precipitated, and in some part created . . . a deleterious effect on mental health."[38]

And that's putting it mildly. The World Health Organization (WHO) reported that the Covid-19 pandemic "triggered a 25% increase in prevalence of anxiety and depression worldwide."[39] Not to mention an uptick in substance abuse,[40] more divorces and breakups,[41] and an intensification of domestic violence to such a degree that violence against women during the pandemic has been called a "shadow epidemic."[42]

It's great that we can get so much work done remotely; I think Woodroffe would agree. But in-person contact leads to an increase in oxytocin (the feel-good hormone), and a decrease in cortisol (the stress hormone). And, unfortunately, digital contact doesn't mirror the neurological benefits of in-person relating. Rather, it adds to our stress and exhaustion by way of that all-too-familiar "Zoom fatigue."[43]

Which is not to say that well-run remote conversations can't create real connections; we've all experienced an amazing video call that made us feel great. It's just important to remember that at the end of the day, no employee is an island.

This is why the C in ACE flexibility stands for *connection*. As the proverbial watercooler interactions become less frequent, we have to be intentional about connecting with one another. These days, our work lives must be planned with face-to-face connection top of mind.

All too often, hybrid work solutions end up with what Drew Houston, founder and CEO of Dropbox, calls "the worst of both worlds." You return to the office—it's loud, everyone's still on Zoom, and what's worse? "You don't have your snacks or your dogs . . . it's a new circle of hell it's probably best to avoid."[44]

Telling someone that they have to schlep into the office when their key team members and friends aren't there, only to sit in a distracting open-office design so they can engage in a little productivity theater is a recipe for resentment.

Simply bringing people back to the office isn't enough to create connection because we all default to what we know. Instead, we have to plan, reflect, and integrate. In other words, we have to be *strategic*. As NYU School of Professional Studies Professor Anna Tavis notes, "companies will have to create an 'ambiance' designed with workers in mind, much like they already do for customers . . . make the workplace experience 'attractive, dynamic, and magical' to compete with workers' homes."[45]

Global design firm IDEO imagines bringing people into the office with a carrot, not a stick. Paul Bennett, chief creative officer, said in a World Economic Forum interview with Charter's Kevin Delaney, "You've got to make people want to come in versus telling them to come in. And you've got to make coming in as exciting as possible."[46] It's not just about free bagels anymore; now, "Free bagels is the cost of entry." IDEO brings people into the office for two priorities: togetherness (what they call a "boost") and tackling the "gnarliest part of [their] project" together as a team. They've been "bringing together 'gnarliness' and 'boostiness' in equal quantities and then surrounding it with bagels."[47] I love it! They also hold "home weeks" where everyone comes together for contests like DJing and drawing. By gamifying the whole week, they've had employees declare, "This will keep me going for six months."[48] If you ever needed proof that a carrot is better than a stick, this is it.

Let's see how some other incredible companies design workplace connections that can't be found within the comforts of home.

Super Connection Days to the Rescue

One way to curate in-person connection is to design a day in the office worth the commute, which I wrote about in an article for *Harvard Business Review* called "In the Hybrid Era, On-Sites Are the New Off-Sites."[49]

When I met Reuben Daniels, managing partner of EA Markets (EA), he was in the process of getting rid of the physical office, but he knew how important it was to replace it with something for his employees to be in person together—to connect. So, he came up with the idea of creating a monthly "Superday." And Daniels asked me to help design the program, which would be a day that employees could consider worth the commute.

We decided to design EA's Superdays around their values of health, wealth, and growth. Each month, when employees got together, they would connect around one or more of the following three values and receive related content:

- Health, which includes flexible office choices, commute limits, and team-building, as well as taking care of employees' wellness
- Wealth, which includes cross-functional meetings, sprint-like work sessions, and team lunches and events
- Growth, which is the time for personal and professional development (which you'll read all about in Chapter Five)

So at EA, we made sure that growth isn't an afterthought. During Superdays, employees connect and learn together through activities like book clubs, speakers, and lunch and learns. And the best part? It's baked right into the middle of the day because it's something EA should—and does—value.

I caught up with Daniels a year later and asked him how Superdays were going. He said that they were going strong and that the only thing they needed was more of them.

Perla Bernstein, EA chief of staff, shared that they added a special Superday in Florida for employees to work, connect, bond, and enjoy some warm weather. During this Superday, which was actually a few days, employees did a deep dive on one topic, The EA Way. Bernstein described it as "a little bit of culture and a little bit of processes and defining how we do what we do. People enjoyed the change of scenery, doing a deep dive, thinking big picture versus business as usual."[50]

There is nothing business as usual about Superday, which is why people want more of them!

Working in the Schools (WITS) is an incredible organization that builds foundational literacy skills for thousands of Chicago Public School students each academic year by connecting mentors from hundreds of Chicago corporations with students in their neighborhood schools. Since its first corporate program in 1999, WITS has been encouraging the Chicago workforce to help meet the literacy needs of elementary schools in underfunded communities across Chicago on the foundation that "reading matters."

Clearly, what they do is good for the world, but could it be a reason to come back into an office to connect with colleagues? As WITS CEO Tena Latona shared with me:

> When it was time to return to in-person programming in September 2022 we knew we were doing so in a new corporate landscape. Our model relied on employees being at their desks in offices in the Loop. That wasn't the case anymore. But we knew our mission mattered to the thousands of mentors that work with our students. So we made WITS a carrot for our corporations. Don't bring people to the

office to fiddle with Excel all day. Bring them to the
office to engage with each other, with their broader
community. That is what WITS has always been—but
it is more relevant now than ever.[51]

Here's how it works: corporations partner with WITS in one of two ways: employees get on a bus to go to meet students in their neighborhood schools or the students come to the office. In both cases, employees get the opportunity to give back, but also connect and engage with colleagues across rank and department.

Patrick Hatton, area vice president of operations for Hyatt, described what it's like when WITS team members leave their Chicago Athletic Association hotel on Michigan Avenue (across from Millennium Park), and get on the bus to see their students:

On the day and time leading up to WITS, there is a
moment of panic. "Can I step away for this today?"
(We always do.) So, we wrap up and walk the four
blocks to catch the yellow bus to school. The bus is
silent on the drive as people are heads down sending
out last-minute emails. Once we arrive at school, our
moods and focus change and we spend the next
45 minutes talking, drawing, laughing, and reading
with our student.

After we say our goodbyes (that sometimes include
a big hug from the student), we load back on
the yellow bus for the journey back to work. The
conversation on the bus on the way back to the
office is 180 degrees different. Mentors are sharing
stories about their experience with their student.

*"Today we just colored." "Mine is a great reader."
Sometimes the kids bring up hard topics that the
team can't imagine, turning the conversation more
serious. It's special to hear the team talk through and
process these moments together. The conversation
continues on the walk back to the office, to the
lunchroom, and on throughout the day. Everyone in
the whole office feels the energy and understands
the value of the program and their impact. It's
contagious!*[52]

In contrast to Hyatt, financial firm William Blair has
another approach: students come to their offices. Stephanie
Braming, global head of investment management at William
Blair, shared with me the impact and connection to their corporate mission:

*Engaging with our communities is one of the three
pillars of our firm's mission. As our team has flexed
to a combination of in-person and remote work, we
have reoriented our days—leveraging the best of
in-person engagement with deep work remotely.
Community engagement is an important ingredient
in our in-person strategy; our philanthropy is 100%
employee-inspired and employee-led. Taking time
out of our day to work with the WITS scholars, seeing
other colleagues who are giving their time as well—it
is a perfect example that we are living our mission.
Reading with and mentoring the scholars brings
our colleagues together, helps us think outside of
ourselves, and is another reason to come to the office
because that is where the kids are!*[53]

What a perfect example of something that's good for people, great for business, and does change the world!

Another company looking for ways to make flexibility work by curating connections is CS Recruiting, a 40-person supply chain recruiting firm run by Charlie Saffro. As offices started reopening in 2021, Saffro did some surveying and found that most of her employees preferred working from home. She decided to buy out their lease and made an intentional decision to use a portion of their rent savings to bring their people together in very specific ways.

Here's how they do it: first, they have four in-person events (one per quarter), where employees come together to have fun, celebrate each other, and connect.

Here's the sweetest part: the day *before* the event, the whole company participates in a two-hour virtual quarterly review to look at the financials and do the "boring" stuff. That way, when they're all together the next day, they can have fun and make it "worth the commute." They plan activities for the day, like bringing in an improv instructor or an author for team building. It's an intentional celebration all about connecting and bonding, which is exactly what a flex culture needs.

CS also uses the money they save on rent to host an annual retreat to a tropical location in February, which is pretty great when your company is based in Chicago! Every single detail of the retreat is designed for connection. As Saffro shared, "We choose the seats at dinner, there's an icebreaker on every table, we pair people up for [our own version of] the Olympic Games on the beach with people who don't normally work together."[54]

It might seem silly to pay so much attention to all the little details, but if you're going to spend the money on a team trip, it will definitely pay off. As Saffro told me, "It's hard to calculate the ROI . . . [but] not a weekend goes by that I don't see photos of people at CS choosing to hang out together, going on a girls' trip . . . two people got married!"[55]

Connections at work have always been the secret sauce of a thriving culture, but in today's flexible workplace, it's a nonnegotiable. You have nothing to lose and much to gain by taking a look at the ways people in your company already love to connect, and just turning up the volume on those activities. Resist the urge to think that if your employees enjoy something, it can't be good for business! Quite the opposite is true. When it comes to making connections, start with what works.

Equity: Beyond Black and White Thinking

Before deep diving into all the research about the Retention Revolution for this book, I probably would have thought that a section on equity—the final piece of our ACE model—in this chapter would be about how important it is to give everyone equal access to remote work.

If the lifestyles of the rich and flexible days meant that only those at the top of the ladder were able to call in from anywhere, wouldn't the Retention Revolution insist that everyone should have the opportunity to call in?

Well, yes and no.

As illustrated in a 2022 McKinsey report, "Hybrid work also has the potential to create an unequal playing field and to amplify in-group versus out-group dynamics, which can flip those advantages to the liabilities side of the ledger." Pretty interesting, huh? The study continues, "For workplaces already challenged to diversify and retain employees, adopting ill-conceived hybrid work models could instead speed departures, decrease inclusion, and harm performance."[56]

In the Retention Revolution, nothing is black and white.

In other words, in order to ACE flexibility, there is no such thing as absolute equity; instead, it's always relative. Nothing will be perfectly equitable for everyone, but your job as a leader is to know how to consider the elements and how they all work together.

And all eyes are on you.

Because of all the complicated equations around the risk and benefits of flexibility for different groups of people, leaders need to talk the talk, walk the walk, and work from home if the company's flexible policy calls for it. If leaders regularly go into the office when the policy is that only a couple in-office days are required each week, employees will feel pressured to go in, regardless of what they really want and what works for them—a serious recipe for resentment.

That's why smart executives, like Anu Bharadwaj, president of Atlassian, understand that to lead by example actually means to hold herself to stricter rules. She explains:

Even after it was deemed safe to return to the office, we decided executives would not go in for more than one day each week and would not hold in-person meetings, without our extended teams, more than once per quarter, with the exception of social events.[57]

When it comes to women and other marginalized groups, the flexibility math gets even more complicated. A 2022 Pew study reported that, "the pandemic 'shecession' is fading as more women return to jobs across the country, aided by new workplace flexibility that could lock in future increases in female employment."[58]

That same study notes:

> There are about 250,000 fewer mothers of small children at work than before the pandemic, compared with about 190,000 fewer fathers. More than 90% of fathers of small children are employed, a complete recovery to the pre-pandemic share. Mothers, though, still lag their own pre-pandemic employment rate by almost 2 points, at 68.6%.[59]

In other words, women still hold the lion's share of unpaid work in the United States, so telling them they can work from home is both a blessing and a curse. L'Oréal USA CHRO Stephanie Kramer shared with me, "As a proud working mom, I happy-cried when the up-to-two-day-a-week working from home policy was announced early in the pandemic, during the summer of 2020. The fact that it was an option to both put my son on the bus *and* have that Asia call when I needed to, *and* there's no negative to my career was a game changer."[60]

Such policies are certainly a wonderful boon for women like Kramer, though it will be even more impactful when men do the same. While it's no surprise that more women prefer flex work than men,[61] affordable childcare is probably a much more equitable solution to the inequities between genders at work.

In addition to women using their flex time to do more unpaid labor, the risk of falling prey to proximity bias is real.[62] Along with the hard-to-shake belief that employees are only working when you can see them, remote workers are less likely to be promoted. According to a recent study from Envoy, "An astounding 96% of leaders take notice of employees' work contributions more often when employees come into the office versus when they work from home."[63]

While men upped their share of unpaid labor during the pandemic, unfortunately, so did women,[64] regardless of job title, income, or education, according to one study from Oxfam and the Institute for Women's Policy Research (IWPR).[65] Flexible work policies will only help women advance if men also take the opportunity to work from home *and* take care of family obligations. And if leaders check their proximity bias at the (office) door.

It's no surprise that, as research from Future Forum shows, "women, employees of color, and working mothers are most likely to want to continue to work flexibly, while men, white employees, and non-caregivers are more likely to go back into the office full-time."[66] This is why it's so important for leaders to be aware of all the nuances of this issue, lest they continue the inequities they're striving to end.

Eve Rodsky, author of *Fair Play*, advises that managers stop giving out assignments—both promotable and nonpromotable—based on gendered assumptions, and instead move to more structured decision-making.

The classic example is the man who, if there's a choice, goes to the office, runs into the boss, and gets a great assignment based on proximity bias, while a woman in that same company takes flex to work from home and receives no special treatment—or her contributions are perceived as less valuable. While more promotable assignments have historically been given to men, nonpromotable tasks—like note taking, ordering the boss's cake, parties, Zoom happy hours, and the like—are more often distributed to women. Rodsky told me a story of a literal rocket scientist who was assigned to pick out the new office floor tile instead of hiring a professional designer because "they assumed that she somehow knows decor better than the men engineers on her team."[67]

To address this unequal distribution of unpaid labor tasks in the workplace, some companies have adopted Rodsky's Fair Play method. They start by examining all their nonpromotable tasks, and instead of giving those tasks to women by assumption and default, they've switched to a round-robin method of structured decision-making. Once all the nonpromotable tasks have been more equitably distributed, then a team can look at their prime assignments in a more intentional way, through the lens of DEI.

And PS: the firm mentioned prior ended up hiring an interior designer so none of the engineers had to pick out floor tile!

This is not to say that flex-for-all is the problem, but leaders have work to do before it's equitable.

Charter, a next generation media and insights company, has embraced the concept of flex from day one. When they started the company, cofounders Kevin Delaney and Erin Grau asked themselves, "What kind of company do we want to be?" They wanted to create a place where people felt happy and cared for.

So, what did that look like in practice? For starters, benefits at Charter are not earned over time. When a new hire joins the company, they're enrolled in benefits, like 401(k) matching and healthcare, as soon as possible. But even more impressive is their leave policy. As Grau told me:

> We don't have cliffs on almost anything. So we have
> no cliffs on our parental leave—you do not have
> to earn it. In fact our managing editor, when we
> gave her the offer, she said she was eight months

*pregnant. And we said to her, "Okay you have access
to parental leave, you don't have to earn it. Tenure
doesn't earn you parental leave. You get it by being
an employee and growing your family." So she had
the full parental leave from six weeks into working at
Charter, which to be honest is hard to do when you're
a startup. To have 12 weeks of parental leave for
employee number five is really, really hard. But it was
a choice because those are our values.[68]*

This perfectly summarizes leaders living by their values.
Even, and especially, when it's hard.

It was one of the reasons Sarah Janowsky, head of business operations, joined Charter. Janowsky left a six-week
sabbatical on the table (which she had earned over five years),
for the flexibility and autonomy she'd be given at Charter
from day one.

As an organization that researches workplace insights,
Charter is also well aware that employees want flexibility
and autonomy, which is why they don't institute strict policies, but rather, give their people guardrails. Grau shared
their philosophy: "Use your best judgment. We hired a
grown-up, and you have great judgment."[69] In the same vein,
they understand that their employees are full humans, many
of whom hold caregiving responsibilities. One of the ways
they bring their human to work is by having employees use
a "heart with caregiving" on Slack to indicate that they're
caregiving, whether for themselves or for someone else. Grau
told me, "You can see it throughout the day, people use it
all the time."[70] I love that they keep caregiving up-front and
don't hide it. People shouldn't have to pretend they're not
parents or caregivers at work.

With the ability to work from home and avoid treacherous commutes, and the accessibility that offers, the *New York Times* reported an increase in employment for disabled people at a rate higher than pre-pandemic levels: "More than 35 percent of disabled Americans ages 18 to 64 had jobs in September [2022]. That was up from 31 percent just before the pandemic and is a record in the 15 years the government has kept track."[71]

Finally, study after study has found that people of color and other marginalized groups are more productive when working from home and prefer doing so at higher rates than their white counterparts.[72] One robust twitter thread with tens of thousands of likes started by Joi Childs opened like this:

"I feel like we don't talk enough about the benefits of working from home as a person of color. Especially because we have to deal with the micro aggressions that come with 'office culture.' "[73]

The thread was so impactful, the *Washington Post* summarized[74] employees' complaints:

- Having colleagues touch their hair
- Being mistaken for another colleague of the same race (a problem solved with names displayed in video meetings)
- Overhearing insensitive commentary on (or being pressured to discuss) traumatizing news events such as racist violence or coronavirus outbreaks in their home country
- Fielding comments from passersby on their "angry" (actually focused) expressions

In this case, remote work isn't the problem, but the workplace is.

While we certainly need to make every effort to create equity for women, people of color, and all manner of socially marginalized groups, we also need to remember that true diversity comes from inviting a variety of viewpoints, neurotypes, and personalities to the table, too. And by making sure they are seen and heard, whether they are in the office, at home, or anywhere in between.

Flexibility is here to stay and it is not just for senior-level desk workers. It's for everyone. But to make flexible work *work* for your teams, you'll need to design it through the lens of autonomy, connection, and equity.

Because if you ACE flexibility, you are one step closer to *ACE*ing the human workplace—for all.

That's a (W)RAP

Retention Action Plan for Flexibility

1. Reflect on your current policies and position around flexible work. Do employees have some autonomy over how, when, and even where they work, whenever possible? Consider your policies through the lens of equity and inclusion, as those wanting flexible work arrangements are often women, caregivers, people of color, and those with disabilities.

2. Whatever gets measured gets managed. Focus on results and outcomes rather than keystrokes or face time. Getting on the same page with how work gets measured will lead to increased trust, combat proximity bias, and make life much easier for managers. Oh—and lose the productivity paranoia! It is not good for anyone.

3. Curate connection whenever employees get together (IRL or virtually). If your employees are commuting into the office, make sure there is a purpose, whether that is to bond, innovate, collaborate, or learn, because employees coming into an empty office just to sit on video calls all day is a recipe for resentment. Design days in the office that are "worth the commute."

4. Provide guardrails to help employees succeed in a flexible environment. Some examples: try implementing core work hours where people are available to each other, asynchronous weeks, or full days without meetings. These types of guardrails, protocols, or rules of the road are critical to implementing a successful flex program for all.

5. Experiment! Solicit feedback from employees. In this new world of work, be open to trying new ways of working, adjusting, and iterating until you find a solution for your organization. But don't get attached because everything's changing.

CHAPTER THREE

THERE IS NO CURTAIN

The Case for Human Professionalism

> **OLD IDEA #3**
>
> "Human professional" is an oxymoron.
>
> **NEW BEGINNING #3**
>
> Professionalism infused with authenticity is the hallmark of today's workplace.

Ellie Middleton of Manchester, England, considers the day she was diagnosed with autism her light bulb moment. And since that life-changing day during the UK's second lockdown, she's been on a mission to make "a lot of noise about neurodiversity" and become a champion for a truly accepting, human world of work.

Ellie's first LinkedIn post on the topic went so viral she was invited on bestselling author Adam Grant's *WorkLife* podcast to discuss it.[1] She's been named one of the "Top 50 Influential Neurodivergent Women in 2022," and she's since become a consultant, speaker, and leader of the un(masked) community.[2]

Her original post[3] (accompanied by a cute selfie, of course) is such an incredible time stamp of our moment, it's worth quoting in its entirety:

> *Can we pls talk for a minute about the outdated idea of what is/isn't "professional"...*
>
> *Things that DON'T make me any less professional:*
>
> 👶 *The fact that I'm young, bubbly and chatty*
>
> 📱 *The fact that I post personal things on social media*

🧠 *The fact that I'm open about my mental health/ neurodiversity*

🪶 *The fact that I have tattoos and a nose ring*

👕 *The fact that I'd rather wear ripped jeans than a suit*

🍸 *The fact that I enjoy letting my hair down on a weekend*

😊 *The fact that my posts are always laced with emojis*

Things that DO make me professional:

🖤 *I love my job and put my all into my work*

✨ *I'm passionate and let my sparkle shine through*

✅ *I'm reliable and get my work done*

📈 *I have *big* goals and I'm building a personal brand*

👫 *I've built great relationships with my team and look forward to building them with clients*

Welcome to the *new* era of professionalism—it's so great to have you here.

Thanks, Ellie! We are happy to have *you* here 🥳🥳🥳!

It's not news that remote work has completely blurred the lines between work and home. Or that because of this shift, the nature of our work may seem to be more *casual*, shall we say, but—by some measures—even more productive and engaged. The WFH Research project, run by Stanford, the University of Chicago, ITAM, and MIT, found in their

"Survey of Working Arrangements and Attitudes" that "people who worked remotely at least some of the time reported being about 9 percent more efficient working from home than they were working from the office."[4] The fact that over the course of the pandemic we ran reports, teams, whole companies—in fact the biggest economies in the world—from our closets, kitchens, and home offices in our jammies has called into question everything we thought we knew about what it means to be a professional.

Author-entrepreneur dynamic duo Sunny Bonnell and Ashleigh Hansberger write in *Fast Company* about senior executives formerly incited not just by fear, but envy and awe:

> No one is buying the act anymore. We've seen your home office and your deck on Zoom, and while they're swank, we've also seen you in your workout shorts and your morning stubble. We've seen your sink piled with dishes, heard your teenager swearing at Instagram, and watched your cat step in front of the screen and stamp its paws all over your T-shirt. You're no longer the Wizard of Oz; there is no curtain.[5]

There's no curtain; the emperor has no clothes; the jig is up.

After spending much of 2020 and 2021 with our kids, spouses, roommates and messes awkwardly on display, it's time to stop hiding. Forget about the elephant in the room; let's take a moment to name the *human* in the room.

Or should I say—on the Zoom!?

We exist, and we're complicated. And we're not always totally "professional."

And that's good news. For us as people, and for our businesses.

Which is why there's never been a better time to unpack the very concept of professionalism. Now is our opportunity to preserve everything that supports innovation, creativity, and life-affirming productivity, while letting go of outdated, unrealistic, and unattuned notions of the sacrifices we have to make in order to succeed—as companies and as individuals.

According to Merriam Webster, a *professional* is defined as "exhibiting a courteous, conscientious, and generally businesslike manner in the workplace."[6] This definition isn't so far off from Ellie's "young, bubbly, and chatty" version of being "reliable," having "*big goals*," and building "great relationships," except for one thing: the whole "generally businesslike manner in the workplace" idea.

So, what does it really mean to behave in a "generally businesslike manner in the workplace"?

Well, it used to mean one thing. But for some people (like Ellie and her peers), it's starting to mean something else.

The way I see it, creating an inspiring space for the human professional comes down to paying attention to how we dress and express for truly human success. I'll explore each of these ideas as well as share one of my favorite case studies of success. As we know from the research, cultivating psychologically safe spaces leads to "higher levels of engagement, increased motivation to tackle difficult problems, more learning and development opportunities, and better performance."[7] What's more, Qualtrics found that "Workplace belonging has emerged as the top employee experience driver linked to engagement and well-being. . . . People who feel like they belong are almost three times as likely to have a greater sense of well-being: 78% versus 28%."[8] In other words, creating psychological safety and belonging in the workplace—a.k.a. where people can authentically (and appropriately) dress and express themselves—is good for people *and* business.

Dress for Success

Priya Parker, facilitator, strategic advisor, and author of the bestselling book *The Art of Gathering*, has some thoughtful insights as to what makes a dress code "successful." In her newsletter from October 2022,[9] she illustrates what a dress code that works gets right, including the way such a guardrail can temporarily equalize, prime your guests (or in this case your colleagues), and orient to the purpose of the gathering (a.k.a. your professional setting), among others.

Parker encourages us to consider how a dress code can "impact the tone" and "ground the gathering in purpose." So, if you apply this framework to your workplace, you can see how important it is to decide on a dress code that delights and unites, and gives space for your people to express themselves—if you choose to have one at all. In other words, let go of the default, outdated, old-fashioned ideas of what it means to "dress for success" and open your mind to a new frontier.

I'll go first. I recently had a call with the head of a Fortune 500 company team who had a tattoo on her wrist. Even a couple years ago, this would've surprised me and, to be honest (another quality of the human professional), I might have even judged her for being—I don't know—maybe not serious?

Dare I say, unprofessional?

But not anymore.

In the Retention Revolution, judging by appearances is being replaced by an appreciation of character.

Why should we pay so much attention to the ways we dress, including the ways other people dress, and our reactions to it? Because of all the ways unconscious—and conscious!—bias can sneak into our dress codes and workplace policies, that's why.

Let's take my previous example and the growing acceptance of tattoos in the workplace as one simple marker of the shift in what it means to dress for success. A 2022 study in the *Journal of Organizational Behavior* found that while people do hold some negative stereotypes about people with tattoos, customers "did not display more negative attitudes or behaviors toward tattooed (vs. non-tattooed) employees," and in some cases, particularly, "in white-collar jobs that involve artistic skills," tattooed employees were viewed more favorably.[10]

Plus, research from LinkedIn shows, "about 60% of working Americans say that the definition of what's considered 'professional' has changed since the start of the pandemic, with the vast majority saying it's changed for the better."[11] Additionally, "the study showed that Gen Z is least likely to believe in the 'traditionally professional' look in the office—less than 40% of workers in the group think you need to maintain a 'conservative' appearance that includes keeping tattoos covered."[12]

As Lindsey Pollak shared in her book *The Remix: How to Lead and Succeed in the Multigenerational Workplace*, changing employee demographics requires leaders to rethink old policies. Two major healthcare organizations recently changed their dress code policies to adapt to the reality of today's workers: Indiana University (IU) Health, a nonprofit healthcare system that includes 16 hospitals, and the prestigious Mayo Clinic both announced that they would now allow nurses to have visible tattoos, which were previously forbidden.

Why the change? Demographics. An estimated 47 percent of millennials in the United States have at least one tattoo, compared to 36 percent of Gen Xers and 13 percent of baby boomers. And this statistic doesn't only refer to potential job candidates. One nurse at IU Health commented that being able to show her tattoos had a positive impact on her relationship with patients, because so many of them had tattoos, too.

Tattoos are prevalent among the younger Gen Z cohort as well. When Pollak asked a summer camp director why his camp eliminated its policy requiring staff (mostly teenagers) to cover their tattoos, he said, "Because if I didn't change that policy, I wouldn't have any staff to hire."[13]

I understand that all this emphasis on how we adorn ourselves might seem a little silly or professionalism-lite. After all, social mores and trends are . . . very human. Who cares? Well, sometimes the most innocent-seeming codes of conduct have complex origins and create an unsafe environment for many people, especially underrepresented groups.

It's true that the pandemic has put the pressure on all of us to question many of these so-called professional ideals, but even before Covid, many people began questioning the expectations to adhere to "business beauty standards." For instance, Black women who were subtly (and not so subtly) told their natural hair had no place at work began standing up against this racist—there's really no other word for it—standard.[14] What can one's hair *possibly* have to do with one's ability to get the job done?

In the Retention Revolution there is absolutely no tolerance for blind adherence to uninformed, old ways of doing business. In 2019, California was the first state to pass a law banning natural hair discrimination; many states have followed suit.[15] As authors Zuhairah Washington and Laura Morgan Roberts write in *Harvard Business Review*, "Women of color don't need to be told to 'lean in.' Research shows that the vast majority of them have confidence and ambition, determination and desire. What they don't always have is managers who understand how to help them overcome all the obstacles that stand in their way."[16]

Yet another reason why in the Retention Revolution, managers absolutely must be coached in the nitty-gritty, human ways to support everyone on their teams.

Though people—and especially women—of color have experienced intense scrutinization regarding their appearance in the workplace, rules about dressing for success are something we all contend with, to varying degrees. The fact that all women have been under tremendous pressure to spend money on clothes, wear uncomfortable shoes, keep up with expensive grooming, and keep their lipstick fresh in order to compete with men—all while continuing to be paid less and work more—is so obvious it's *almost* too cliché to even mention. But I'll risk it in the name of making my case for the human professional.

In his book *Dress Codes: How the Laws of Fashion Made History*, Stanford Law Professor Richard Thompson Ford writes, "Expressive fashions have been used to symbolize social status, political affiliation, individual personality, and, of course, gender for centuries."[17] From the business suit to the power hoodie, and most recently, as Ford writes, the "Zoom shirt [that] we put on over our PJs for meetings at the beginning of the pandemic," we just can't help ourselves from dressing to impress. And not just with the clothes we wear. Ford continues, "Another thing that developed [during the pandemic] was a kind of subtle new dress code that involved . . . what was behind you in the room . . . your kitchen, dining room or living room [have become] part of that public persona."[18]

And there we are, full circle, back to the idea of a public—or professional—persona. Because we're social animals, we'll always be on the lookout for ways to fit in, but the truly human way is to take off the pressure and add in some personality. Yes, even—and especially—at work.

I can hear the questions now. Sure, bring your human to work, but how much human is too much? How much of you do your colleagues really want to see? When is it OK to wear a midriff-bearing shirt, or a slogan on a T-shirt, or a sleeve of tattoos? The answer is that it always depends on context, culture, and community. And like with everything else in the Retention Revolution, when in doubt, ask the question. And be willing to listen to the answers.

In other words, have a conversation.

THE **SWEET SPOT**
BETWEEN **TECH & CONNECT**

VILLYGE

In 2001, I was newly married and working in a high-powered job as a consultant, while also managing fertility treatments, a miscarriage, and then, a high-risk twin pregnancy. I wish I'd had access to technology to help me to feel seen, supported, and human.

Every day, I tried to keep a brave face in the office and in front of my two male bosses, hoping nobody would notice me coming in late because I had to stop by the fertility clinic to have my blood levels checked. While the medical appointments were tiring, what was truly exhausting was the energy it took to hide what was going on behind the scenes.

What if there had been an easy way to share what was going on in my life?

What if there had been a tool to help my bosses better support me in my specific situation?

Fast-forward 20 years. Entrepreneur Debi Yadegari has created such a tool after "trading her briefcase for a diaper bag" because she felt so incredibly unsupported as a nursing mom in her job as a Wall Street lawyer. As every parent knows, it takes a village to raise your kids; as Yadegari has made it clear, it takes a Villyge to raise and support professionals in a human-centered way.

And, by the way, according to Yadegari, companies are losing $1 trillion annually from attrition costs and $360 billion annually in lost productivity because managers don't know how to show up for employees in the ways that they need.[19]

This is how it works: Let's say you're delighted to discover that you're pregnant and you know you need to share the news with your manager, but you aren't sure how and when to share the news. How will your manager respond? Will you have the support you need to keep your career moving forward while you grow your family? As Yadegari put it, "Employees want to share with their managers, but there's not always an easy way to do so."[20] Villyge offers a safe, easy, and confidential space to share what's really going on, personally and professionally, all while giving managers the tools necessary to show up for their employees in the ways that matter.

Here's the thing: Employees *want* managers to understand what is going on in their lives. According to a Villyge survey, 100 percent of employees said they would share *more* if they knew their manager was receiving guidance to help support them.[21] And bringing smart tech to the table is a great way to make that very human connection.

After all, it takes a Villyge to raise a human professional.

Express for Success

When I was rising up the ranks as a workplace strategist and consultant, the idea of bringing your whole self to work was pretty ridiculous. Even in 2017, when I interviewed people for my book *Bring Your Human to Work*, many asked if I was talking about bringing my (very human) dog, Cruiser, to work. I still get that question! Bringing yourself to work, especially for leaders and managers, was a no-no. Across the board, big feelings had no place in the office.

These days, while certainly the tides are shifting, I'm still often asked, "Should I really, *really* bring my whole self to work? How much expression is too much?"

I'm so glad you asked.

If you were on LinkedIn at all in August 2022, you'll likely remember the CEO of a small B2B marketing and sales agency who became the face (literally) of oversharing at work. This CEO posted a photo of himself on LinkedIn with tears streaming down his face over having to lay off 2 of his 17 employees. This became such a *thing* that the *New York Times* covered it in an article called, "When Your Boss Is Crying, but You're the One Being Laid Off."[22]

Oof.

Even before the article ran, this post received 10,000 comments, some in favor, certainly, but many more criticizing the way his post drew all the attention toward himself and his pain, instead of toward the people who lost their jobs. And there were lots of comments like this: "A very unprofessional performance here."

Yes, we want room for human expression. But too much of a good thing is . . . sometimes *not* so good.

One of the most beloved business books to come out in the past several years was *No Hard Feelings: The Secret Power of Embracing Emotions at Work* by Liz Fosslien and Mollie West Duffy, known affectionately to their (as of June 2023) 566 thousand Instagram followers as @lizandmollie. This is a groundbreaking exploration of what it means to be human at work. And it's a pleasure to read!

In 2022, the pair came out with *Big Feelings: How to Be Okay When Things Are Not Okay*, which was—like their first book—a *Wall Street Journal* bestseller and celebrated by the *New York Times*, NPR, and *Good Morning America*, to name a few. Which is to say, while we have a ways to go to figure out exactly how much human we should be bringing to work, there's no going back. I consider this a good thing.

Great, you might say, bring all the feelings. But what does this have to do with the Retention Revolution?

Pew Research Center discovered that for the workers who quit their jobs in 2021, 57 percent said feeling disrespected was a reason why they quit, falling just behind the top two reasons: low pay (63 percent) and a lack of opportunities for advancement (also 63 percent).[23] If you ask me, these are all just ways of saying an employee is not being respected enough.

Employees will leave your company if they don't feel respected as people, which includes respecting their feelings.

And they won't be coming back.

Study after study shows that people want and need to express themselves. A lot. During the pandemic, Edelman found that 63 percent of employees asked for daily feedback, and 20 percent wanted communication several times a day![24] Though sometimes you might feel repetitive or like a broken record, trust me . . . there's a certain, very human, charm to a broken record.

One of the greatest gifts from the pandemic is the ubiquitous check-in, that totally earnest, "How are you, really?" that people were asking each other, especially at the beginning of virtual meetings and events. Well guess what? We need to keep doing it.

So, don't worry about going overboard. When in doubt, communicate, communicate, communicate.

Up Your Check-In Game

The check-in might not dazzle from afar, but once you look closely, you'll see how this is a remarkably simple, accessible way for leaders to show their interest, benefit from human connection, and support the humans they work with.

Leaders at Mars Veterinary Health-owned Banfield Pet Hospital, the leading provider of preventive veterinary care with more than 1,000 hospitals nationwide and 20,000 associates, are urged to take their check-ins seriously. And in an industry facing higher-than-average mental health challenges and high rates of suicide among veterinarians, it's even more crucial. Check out this extremely simple but powerful tip from Melissa Marshall, vice president of people and organization: "At Banfield, we believe that cultivating help-seeking behaviors among staff is key to creating a culture of well-being and an environment where people feel comfortable with regular and honest check-ins," says Marshall. "One of my biggest tips is for leaders to prioritize going to where the conversation is happening instead of expecting the conversation to come to us. For our hospital staff, that's often in their daily huddle."[25]

So, what happens in these daily huddles?

According to Mars chief medical officer, Molly McAllister, Doctor of Veterinary Medicine, Banfield begins by using "huddle cards," which cover a range of topics including health and well-being, equity, inclusion and diversity, and clinical skills to guide the discussion. Leaders are better equipped to help educate people on why health and well-being are important; help them discover where they are focusing their emotional, mental, and physical energy in their personal lives and with their teams; and give them the language and tools to bring it to life in their practice on a regular basis.

Then, Banfield leaders ask their teams: "How are you *really* doing?"

Importantly, Banfield's daily (and sometimes multiple times a day) huddles are "not a time to inform [the staff] of the newest corporate policy. It *really* is a check-in," notes McAllister. And this is very important. Huddles offer "that environment of safety to share what you need to share, promote the quality of care we provide our pets, and promote their own sense of self and well-being in that environment."[26]

By supporting doctors and hospital teams through daily, intentional check-ins, they are able to better focus on providing patient care.

Donald Knight, chief people officer of Greenhouse, is one of those human leaders who "gets it." He approaches his one-on-one meetings as an opportunity to check in and learn more about a person, connect authentically, and create a safe space to share what's working and what isn't. To do this, he asks the question, "What is throwing you off your game?"

When I asked him about this very human approach, he said, "That's one of the easiest ways to prioritize connection. Because it allows the opportunity to demonstrate vulnerability around what's not necessarily going well."[27] Even when what is not going well has to do with Knight himself!

Knight gave an example from his own team: when he asked the question, "What is throwing you off your game?" to one of his leaders, the leader responded with, "Well, there's an opportunity for you, Don, to live well-being more. We feel like we have to be on all the time because you're on all the time." That led Knight—someone who tends to be up at odd hours of the day—to practice better habits around communication, like delaying sending messages until work hours. When he goes on vacation, he completely unplugs and gives his team a recap when he returns on how he prioritized his own well-being. The leader who brought this to Knight's attention thanked him and said he now can demonstrate to his own team that "when we're on we're on, and when we are off, we are completely off."[28]

Another way companies have been institutionalizing a real, human check-in is through a "red, yellow, green" system, like the one Reboot uses at the beginning of meetings. Green means all is well; yellow indicates manageable stress;

red is alert. And importantly, "The goal isn't to be green. The goal is to be honest."[29]

Finally, if you want to get really wild with your check-in, you can be like the folks at Mural, a digital workspace for visual collaboration, and "Pick Your Nic."

Yep, you read that right.

At Mural, they have a meeting check-in called *Pick Your Nic.* Invented by former employee Erica Green, each person picks from a selection of images of . . . wait for it . . . Nicholas Cage . . . that best represents how they are feeling that day. Options include happy, carefree, relaxed, excited, focused, stressed, angry, bees!!!, and meh!

Why Nicolas Cage? Sure, he's played a lot of characters in his career, spanning lots of different moods, feelings, and emotions, but ultimately, it doesn't really matter how people come together to express themselves. What matters is that they're invited to do so.

And sometimes, the tables turn. One of my favorite DEI experts is Daisy Auger-Dominguez, chief people officer at Vice Media, Inc. In a LinkedIn post from October 2022, she talks about a surprising turn of events during a check-in:

> In a recent 1:1 with one of my direct reports, I was caught off guard when they asked, "How are YOU?" I was focused on coaching them through a rough spot. Turning that conversation into a shared moment of contemplation grounded us differently. I admitted to also feeling tired—who isn't? I also shared a few of the practices that I've been leaning on to keep me centered and focused on what's most important for our teams. That includes new ways of figuring out how to solve the urgency of the "now" with a lens on

*equitably designing "what's next" and giving myself
grace when I don't get it right.*

*The generosity of that comment filled me with
gratitude as a co-worker and a manager. It also
reminded me how easy it can be to turn a seemingly
routine conversation into a meaningful one.*[30]

People, this isn't rocket science but it does require some
serious intention. To create a human-friendly culture of warm
connection that doesn't become TMI (aka Too Much Information) for your teams, it is important to remember that
some people prefer to keep their business and personal lives
separated. And that's OK, too. It has to be! People should
never feel pressured to share at work.

Nancy Rothbard, professor at the Wharton School of the
University of Pennsylvania and an expert on emotions at work,
conducted research that confirmed that while there is a "growing expectation that people bring their 'full selves' to work,
prompted by technologies that blur the lines between work and
life . . . surveys indicate that people tend to prefer segmenting
their professional and personal lives instead of integrating
them. But often they don't feel they have the option."

Which is definitely not OK. Being vulnerable at work,
like anything personal, must be a choice, not an expectation.
If it seems impossible to navigate the tricky world of human
expression, you're definitely on the right track.

Wait, did I just say you *should* be confused?

I did.

Because being a human professional is not a straightfor-
ward, box check, one-and-done, spreadsheet-able situation.

So, what's a human professional to do? First of all, slow
down and know that in times like this, experimentation is

the name of the game. You won't always get everything *right*, or make everyone comfortable all of the time. What matters is that you, as the leader, take the time to sensitively explore each question that comes before you with an open mind and on a case-by-case basis. But don't do it alone. It's imperative that you have a diverse group of trusted advisors who can help you learn through these tricky times.

And don't worry, you won't be the sheriff of the Wild West forever! After a few instances of questionable conduct, you'll soon discern a pattern—a culture that works for you and your company will emerge. And you'll look back on these days with pride at how you hung in there and figured it out.

Success!

I'd like to close this chapter with a story that epitomizes the successful human professional leader and workplace of our time.

In 2022, I met Judith Harrison, chief diversity, equity, and inclusion officer at global communications firm Weber Shandwick. After George Floyd's murder, Harrison, hurt and disturbed, decided to offer a time for employees to come together to process their grief. Now, the company holds virtual gatherings once a month—and sometimes more often—in response to traumatic events. Harrison calls this simple circle, "Time to Connect."

Time to Connect has become an important ritual at the company.

How does Harrison do it?

For starters, when employees come together for Time to Connect, Harrison begins with some prepared remarks about the world event and then asks the same question each time: "So, how are you doing?"

In order to give employees permission to answer this question honestly, she opens the conversation with her own thoughts and feelings; she leads the way with just the right amount of vulnerability, enough so employees can feel safe to respond to the conversations in whatever way works for them—whether live (they raise their virtual hand, unmute, and speak to the group), by responding in the chat, or via email after the fact.

And answer honestly, they do.

For instance, after the July 4, 2022, shooting in Highland Park, Illinois, Angela Salerno-Robin, SVP media relations, responded with, "I am not OK." She continued:

> *These sessions are a time for us to support one another and talk in a safe space. This time was different. This time, I was the one who personally needed the support. Highland Park is my home. We moved our family here from Chicago to give our children a "safer" place to grow up. It's hard for me to put into words how we are feeling, but I can tell you that as a family, as a community, and as a nation—we are not OK!*

It's not uncommon for participants to cry and share out loud or via the chat function. They express themselves.

When I asked Harrison about the business results of Time to Connect, she told me, "Based on people's comments about how much they look forward to the calls and how 'therapeutic' they are, I think the business impact is in engagement, with belonging and trust being subsets of this category."[31]

A perfect environment for humans to thrive.

And the best part for anyone still on the fence? Studies show that the kind of experience that Time to Connect inspires—a feeling of cocreation, genuine care, and solidarity—have been found to be closely tied to retention.[32]

It's fascinating to contemplate all the ways professionalism is changing, and to see how norms around expression at work are shifting into the human zone. But, how then do leaders bring all these human professionals together in ways that encourage their collective success?

As you consider ways to operationalize the kind of human professionalism that arose during the pandemic, we certainly don't want to turn back the clock to March 2020. But, we also don't want to forget what we saw and how we felt.

Most of the best practices for integrating new professional norms into your culture are totally accessible. All you need is intention and a good dose of human professionalism.

That's a (W)RAP

Retention Action Plan for Human Professionals

1. Gather your current policies (if any) around dress and expression in the workplace. If you don't have any, now's the time. Reflect on why you have a specific policy in place, if it needs to be changed (or scrapped altogether), and make sure it's inclusive of all your people. Let go of the idea that professionalism equates to looking a specific (read: old-fashioned) way. If any of your policies feel outdated or, frankly, biased against a certain group, adjust.

2. Create a safe workplace for all employees to bring their full selves to work—that is, where people feel free to express themselves in whatever way you deem appropriate (see Number One above). Prioritize psychological safety and belonging at work. That might look like a regular, dedicated meeting, where everyone can share how they're doing and how they can be supported.

3. Check in . . . a lot. Your people want to know that you care about them and that you're focused on their mental, emotional, and physical well-being. Ask your employees, "How are you really, *really* doing?" And then listen to what they tell you.

4. Decide what the right amount of vulnerability looks like for you and each of your direct reports or teammates. Build your emotional intelligence (EQ) and trust, so you know how much sharing is too little or too much. The context and audience matters when sharing parts of yourself.

5. Walk the walk. Leaders are humans, too, and employees want to see their bosses be vulnerable, prioritize their well-being, and model best practices for taking care of themselves.

CHAPTER FOUR

WE HAVE TO STOP MEETING LIKE THIS

The Three P's of Meetings

OLD IDEA #4

Meetings are just . . . what you do.

NEW IDEA #4

Meetings are a critical ingredient in the recipe for retention.

Another great gift from the pandemic is that we now have a lot of options.

When it comes to meetings, this is both a blessing and a curse.

Sometimes meeting in person is just better, or even necessary. Other times, remote meetings are perfect. Hybrid meetings—with some people gathered in person and others remotely—are necessary even if they aren't everyone's favorite. In fact, they can often be the worst of both worlds. The remote participants miss out on the in-person connectivity, and the in-person folks have to tolerate yet another remote meeting. Sure, in some situations, it's great to have it as an option. But as with everything else in the Retention Revolution, what matters most is being intentional—and knowing why you're doing what you're doing.

And maybe you'll find that you don't even have to meet at all.

The past few years have led to seriously seismic shifts in the world of work; we all know that. The tectonic shift to remote work has certainly transformed our day-to-day lives in—until recently—unimaginable ways; it has also given rise to some new ways of working.

One of the biggest paradigm shifts comes from the rise of what's called "asynchronous," or "async," work, which is defined by Nextiva, a remote communication company, as "a method of exchanging information without the expectation of real-time feedback."[1] GitLab, which we've already met, is one of the world's biggest all-remote and truly async companies. They rely on their employees to extensively document every single aspect of their jobs in order to communicate across functions and time zones. Whether you're fully remote, a mix of remote and in person, or even fully in person, adopting an async attitude allows individuals to work deeply on projects and then collaborate by sharing documents. Others can then concentrate on said documents, alone, in their own time, and at their own pace.

This kind of working offline has a huge impact on the ways we meet, even if your entire workforce is, as they say, colocated, that is, all in the same place. It truly is a new world. And the only way to stay ahead in the Retention Revolution is to accept that how you hold meetings has to change.

Nicholas Shiya, former director of real estate advisory at WeWork, a collaborative working space, put it well: "Think of asynchronous work more like a relay than an individual sprint."[2] Which means meetings are kept in reserve for when they're really necessary—either for in-person gatherings, which nobody disputes is vital for every kind of team, by the way, or for something that just can't be done via networks on the cloud.

If you're willing to embrace even the tiniest bit of the async approach, you might start to see meetings like Soulaima Gourani, a founder, investor, speaker, and bestselling author. She writes in *Forbes*, "A fully packed calendar was once a status symbol; today, it is a sign of poor (self) leadership and poor judgment."[3]

Those are some strong words, I know.

But she has a point. Today, there is no reason (or excuse) for the kind of meeting mania that has been haunting companies for years. In 2018, I wrote the following in *Bring Your Human to Work*:

> *Every day in the United States, at least 36 million meetings are held. It's no surprise to anyone that, in many of these meetings, people bring in unrelated work, produce grade-school-worthy doodles, and even catch up on some ZZZs. Each year, we waste an estimated $37 billion on unproductive meetings, with executives spending up to 23 hours of their workweek in meetings.[4]*

Today, according to data from Microsoft, the "time spent in Microsoft Teams meetings has gone up more than 250% since March 2020."[5] And according to the National Bureau of Economic Research, the number of meetings employees attend has increased by 13 percent.[6]

Plus, remote meetings are more prone to lead to serious burnout when compared to in-person meetings because you have to be more *on* during virtual meetings,[7] you have to look at yourself all the time,[8] and you miss out on the mitigating positive effects of watercooler run-ins. Now, sure, you can hide your self-view (so you don't have to stare at yourself all day), get up and move around, reduce your window size, and lots of other small fixes.

But you can also *not* meet.

After all, one oft-repeated statistic in the anti-meeting world (yes, that's a thing) is that "70% of all meetings are a waste of time, 70%!"[9] And bad meetings directly impact how someone feels about his or her job. According to Leadership IQ, 65 percent of people who dislike their jobs report that they're frequently stuck in meetings that are not productive. By contrast, only 24 percent of people who love their jobs say they're frequently in unproductive meetings.[10]

Are you starting to get the picture?

Now, as you could guess, I'm not a fan of canceling all your meetings, but I am a fan of having fewer, more selective and purposeful meetings.

Regardless of where you find yourself on the async spectrum, there is no doubt that the technology that has enabled us to survive (and thrive) since 2020 is the exact same technology that will allow us to rethink how, when, where, why, and with whom we should meet. Because even though some of us on the GitLab side of the debate may opt out of many meetings, most of us will continue the ritualized, if not always *necessary*, practice of meeting. So, it's important that we know how to meet well—and that's what I'll share with you in this chapter—some rules of the road.

What I've discovered over these past few years, through hundreds of my own virtual and hybrid meetings, as well as by working with companies to find their human way in this new world is this: every good meeting—whether it's in person or remote—is good in the same three ways.

The Three P's of good meetings? Purpose, Presence, and Protocols.

Purpose

In 2015, I came across a study[11] that changed my life and my career.

Organization and Management Professor at Cornell University, Kevin Kniffin, was studying what makes one team higher performing than another team. Because his dad was a firefighter, and he had grown up hanging out in firehouses, that's where he did his research. He found that the firefighters who are the most dedicated to the ritual of the firehouse meal perform better, that is, they save more lives.

Pretty incredible, huh?

I was—and still am—deeply inspired by what Kniffin discovered. In fact, I was so moved by the study that I launched the Spaghetti Project, a roving platform that shares the science and stories of connection at work. I've hosted over 100 spaghetti dinners all over the country, with every kind of spaghetti you can imagine—gluten-free, vegetarian, kosher. The Spaghetti Project was even featured in the *New York Times*![12]

And then in March 2020 . . . well, you know what happened.

Spaghetti Projects over Zoom?

Lots of people asked for them, but my heart just wasn't in it. Sure, the technology would have enabled me to get lots of hungry—in many ways—people on a virtual call. I could have invited plenty of folks to pull up a chair and a bowl of their own homemade pasta and connect with each other, and it could have been great! But something stopped me from doing it.

It wasn't that I didn't want to connect with people. In fact, being the extrovert that I am, I craved connection more than ever during the pandemic. But I just knew that the Spaghetti Project on a screen felt—to me—like putting out a fire over Zoom: impossible.

Meanwhile, I was doing lots of online keynotes and fireside chats about how to lead in these turbulent times and how to bring our human to the virtual world. So, it's not that

I didn't embrace the technological options. It's just that not every meeting is created equal.

You have to figure out the purpose of your meeting. My purpose in the Spaghetti Project was to be *with* people—in person. Nothing else would do. But, of course, that's not the case for every meeting.

Jellyvision, a software company you'll meet in a few pages—and then again in the final chapter—launched a "seven-year itch" dinner in 2022 because, as chief of staff Brynn Michelich shared, "they say the love is lost in a relationship after seven years, so we like to celebrate that our employees are still hanging in there with us."[13] In such a case, with a purpose like that, a Zoom call just would not do.

While it might feel counterintuitive to create a very narrow focus of your meetings, the fact is that the more niche you are, the more meaningful experience participants will have. In Priya Parker's bestselling book, *The Art of Gathering*, she writes, "The more focused and particular a gathering is, the more narrowly it frames itself and the more passion it arouses."[14]

For instance, perhaps you and your team meet every Thursday for a marketing meeting—an opportunity to check in on everyone's progress and gather insights from the week. Since you're a distributed team, you meet virtually but some folks are also together in the office. The meeting is booked as an hour on everyone's schedule, so even if you don't have news or action, you always fill the hour with brainstorming about future initiatives, troubleshooting tricky cultural issues, and catching up and chatting, which is important! Since you don't have a shared watercooler experience, this marketing meeting is the perfect place to connect.

Right?

Actually, pretty wrong.

Here's why.

Amy Bonsall, the CEO of Collective, a company devoted to helping remote teams thrive, writes in *Harvard Business Review* that there are three types of meetings (or "gatherings," as she calls them, to get around the whole "people around a conference table" or the online equivalent). They are:

Transactional gatherings, which move work forward

Relational gatherings, which strengthen connections

Adaptive gatherings, which help us address complex or sensitive topics[15]

I love this breakdown and think it can help you decide what kind of meeting you should have. Do transactional meetings need to be in person? Probably not. Can relational meetings be virtual? Maybe! Should adaptive meetings always be in person? Possibly.

Now, the marketing meeting from earlier feels like an unfortunate mix of all three. So, let's see how we might use Bonsall's advice to see what happens to our marketing meeting.

The ostensible purpose is to go over marketing updates, which is transactional. So, if it were my meeting, I might share a document in which we could all update our latest online actions. If something sticky arises out of this async back and forth, we could meet virtually for a quick action-item review.

Assuming everyone lives relatively near each other, I'd make a weekly in-person lunch date when we're all in the office to take care of our very important desire to relate to each other. If you don't live locally, make it virtual and perhaps hold quarterly in-person meetings. Whatever you do, don't leave this out! If you lose connection, you lose the glue that keeps you working well together. Socializing is so important, you need to dedicate specific time just for that.

Next, I'd decide on the best time for the whole team to meet either virtually (with videos on, for those who are willing) or in person to discuss the ongoing tricky issues that arise within our culture. And in the meantime, I'd create a shared doc with specific questions based on the issues people have already mentioned, to keep them top of mind. That way, when we do meet for an adaptive meeting, we'll have an agenda, we'll know who needs to be there (and welcome or even encourage people to leave the meeting when their section is over), and we'll be able to go *much* deeper into an issue than we ever could while talking around the edges of our so-called marketing meeting.

General Mills has a philosophy around flexibility called "Work with Heart." It's a fluid framework by design, creating intentional moments to come together. They understand flexibility is important *and* they also know that in-person moments matter. CHRO Jacqueline Williams-Roll shared, "We made a decision very early on that we were not going to be remote. We think there is power in coming together, but we have to do it intentionally."[16] I couldn't agree more.

Their Work with Heart philosophy is about coming together around four C opportunities: Create, Collaborate, Celebrate, and Connect. But leaders were very clear that when they say "coming together," they don't mean coming *into the office*. Every manager with a team is asked to have a discussion at the individual and collective levels regarding their moments that *matter*. They ask, "When do we need to come together as a team to do one of these four C's?"

This last part is really important: They urged leaders to say to their teams (in their own way, of course), "Let's shake hands on those moments that matter, and let's revisit them every three months because the world is changing, and we will get things wrong." According to Williams-Roll, this approach "conditioned employees from the beginning to let them know that we are going to listen to them, we are going to codevelop solutions with them, and by the way, we are human and [are] going to get things wrong and change."[17]

When we know the *why* of our meeting, the *where* and the *how* become clearer. This is a purpose-first world. But, of course, not every purpose-first meeting needs to be in person—or even singular in its focus.

Connect Up at Upwork

Hayden Brown, the CEO of Upwork, told me about a weekly meeting called "Connect Up" which is an optional 30-minute virtual meeting with their distributed team. It's one of the most well-attended meetings. Though, as Brown told me, the meeting has "only about seven minutes of planned content,"[18] it maintains enough of a structure that people remain engaged.

How?

The meeting has a purpose.

Why would employees with so many other things to do attend yet another virtual meeting when they don't have to?

While the format of the meeting is flexible and "very organic," the purpose of the meeting is to "just have this touchpoint." And that's enough. In order to keep it focused and not just an excuse to meet like in the marketing meeting example earlier, "we use this tool called Slido to collect questions and have people vote on them. That tool is open all week long, so people can ask questions as they come up and vote on them even before the meeting."[19]

By the time everyone meets, the gathering is:

A great connection point, not just for me to answer questions, but also for other leaders to be visible and address things that are going on in the business. And that meeting gets a ton of attendance.

It actually has been growing in attendance over time, which is a great testament, I think, to how people find it really valuable.[20]

Indeed, showing up (with purpose!) is what it's all about.

Connect Out(side) at Cotopaxi

Outdoor gear and clothing brand Cotopaxi has a workforce of 300 people (45 percent of whom are fully remote) spread across a distribution center and 11 retail stores. They host various meetings at a regular cadence, and how and when they gather depends on the meeting's *purpose*.

The "All-Llamas" (a nod to their mascot) is a monthly all-hands-on-deck meeting held Wednesday at noon, where everyone comes together to talk transparently about how the company is doing. Most companies host all-hands, but this one is seriously people-focused. This call includes tons of recognition, the next micro- or macroinvestment the company is making in people (like incremental time off or employee volunteer time), and birthday and anniversary announcements. As Grace Zuncic, chief people and impact officer, shared with me, "It's just more collaborative. It's not like a webinar where the C-suite is coming on and each different C-suite member speaks to their updates, and then the call's over. It feels like you're going to join and be a part of it."[21]

"Life Hikes" are meetings held every other Friday, where an employee can opt in and share their life story. People share emotional stories about topics like losing parents, being adopted, or feeling lost in life—people are very vulnerable. "[Employees] just talk about who they are. It's really powerful, and people enjoy that a lot," Zuncic shared.[22]

For their "Impact in Action" meeting, which is held once a month, Cotopaxi's impact partners are invited to come and talk about their outcomes-based programs to alleviate global poverty and advocate for climate justice—and the role of the Cotopaxi Foundation in advancing this work.

And now for my favorite: the once-a-year, in-person "Summer Camp" meeting. Similar to what you'd expect from the summer camps of youth, employees gather together in the summertime for a campout. It's an optional two days together in the wild, and they have a great turnout, because the camp is scheduled for a time when many hourly workers can make it. What I love most is that the executive team makes breakfast for everyone in the morning. Talk about a breakfast of champions!

As Marissa Magno, vice president, people and inclusion, shared with me, "We've focused on how and when we communicate, as well as why we meet, because we believe our employees need real connection and strong relationships with one another to create belonging."[23] And why does creating a sense of belonging matter so much in the big picture of the Retention Revolution? It's not just a feeling we're looking for here; it's a way of doing business.

Magno puts it well: "The feeling that results from being part of something bigger than oneself and the collective ability to drive purpose and give back in bigger ways has a huge impact on our employees seeing Cotopaxi as their career highlight and [on] our business success."[24]

Using Cotopaxi as your template, think of ways you can leverage what matters most to you and your company and come up with some surprising ways to bring people together. And remember, when you align your meetings with purpose, variety will happen naturally.

THE **SWEET SPOT** BETWEEN **TECH & CONNECT**

PAIRUP

According to US Surgeon General Dr. Vivek Murthy, "Quality social support, social integration, and regular communication among co-workers of all levels are key in preventing chronic work stress and workplace burnout." What's more, "Workplace connectedness is also associated with enhanced individual innovation, engagement, and quality of work."[25] But sadly, according to Gallup's State of the Global Workplace: 2022, "60% of people are emotionally detached at work."[26]

What if people could better access meaningful connections at work by ensuring the right people were "in the room"?

PairUp to the rescue!

PairUp is a digital platform designed to accelerate workplace connection and knowledge sharing by tapping into a company's internal expert network. Harnessing the power of generative AI, the software eliminates inefficiencies, saving companies time and resources lost to silos. With PairUp, employees have easy and personalized access to the networks they need to be successful in their roles. PairUp's AI chatbot, Sam, identifies who employees should be meeting with and what to cover, so that they can get the most out of their time together. When meetings are relevant and productive, people feel more connected and a greater sense of belonging.

Which is exactly what the Retention Revolution is all about.

Vanessa is a new sales manager leading a team of reps within a large global corporation, who felt the pain of inefficient meetings. Because she was on a hybrid team, people didn't know each other and had no sense of who could help them, often wasting hours of time looking for answers on their own. And while meetings were often required at the company, people rarely knew *why* they were meeting, or who else was even on the call.

Sound familiar?

Most people calling in to meetings via Zoom kept their cameras off, and the chat was consistently quiet.

Oof.

PairUp identified connections for Vanessa and her teammates, both within her organization and with other sales departments. Utilizing PairUp's research-backed algorithm, staff were matched with the right help based on their needs, interests, communication styles (Wow!), and goals—and then were given context around what to talk about and how to best support each other—making the most out of their meeting time.

As a result, the flow of knowledge sharing, awareness of roadblocks, and access to social connections improved in meetings. Another employee, Peter, used PairUp to connect with three other team members who were selling to similar regions, and who also happened to be new parents like himself. The intentional conversations they had helped Peter learn from their market experiences and feel a greater sense of commonality and connection with his team (and less alone as a parent).

PairUp's research-backed smart technology leverages generative AI to seed a near-instant culture of support, and invites people to be truly human.

Presence

If the purpose is clear, your next step will be to ensure that people show up.

Literally and figuratively.

These days, because it's so incredibly easy for people to slip through the virtual meeting cracks, you might want to consider designating a person whose job it is to cruise direct, if you will. Think Julie McCoy meets the Retention Revolution.

One big question: Who's in charge of managing the ungainly schedules of hybrid work with the added responsibility of planning events or activities for people to connect, both IRL and virtually? This role is called many things: connection curator, people coordinator (Meetup), workplace manager (Jellyvision), head of workplace experiences (Qualtrics), workplace operations manager (Greenhouse), and community manager (Dropbox), to name a few.

Whatever you want to call it, it's a dedicated role to meet this unique, pandemic-induced shift in the way we work and connect. This person's job is to design for connection, own it, iterate and adapt (especially as the way we work continues to shift and change), and—critically—look at it through the lens of diversity, equity, and inclusion. Which is to say, this connection curator role needs to be an explicit part of someone's current job or even a new job entirely because left to our own devices, it won't happen. And that's bad for business.

Making Jellyvision Fun Again

Amanda Lannert, CEO of Jellyvision, a Chicago-based software company, talked to me about what happened to their "crazy in-person culture" during the pandemic and their shift to remote work, including one way they've taken steps to reestablish presence through meetings:

> That day-to-day closeness and intimacy of lunches and watercooler and drinks and non-Zoom camaraderie died during the pandemic. And so work [became] just work. And I really think that the most important thing Jellyvision's doing right now is getting coworkers together to **not** work, to actually be human, because that's where trust comes in and loyalty comes in. People aren't loyal to companies,

people are loyal to people; people aren't inspired by companies, largely they're inspired by people and we've lost a lot of humanity.[27]

So, what's the solution?

Have someone *own* connection.

Meet Brynn Michelich, who has been with Jellyvision for 15 years, supporting Lannert in a variety of different roles. During the pandemic, she was promoted to chief of staff, where a large part of her job became, according to Lannert, "help[ing to] curate events that build intimacy and trust and are productive and, you know, fun."[28]

Michelich shared with me that when Jellyvision was able to start having events again in 2021, the default was that every event had both an in-person and a virtual component. It didn't work, was the worst of both worlds, and definitely not "fun." So, Michelich and her team made some changes.

First, they decided that all of Jellyvision's town hall meetings would be held virtually because who needs to be in-person together to look at screens? Not me!

Second, they launched monthly get togethers—some virtual and others fully in person. While Jellyvision will cover the travel costs for anyone who lives out of town for these in-person events, they are not mandatory. Michelich noted:

> *There is always an in-person quarterly event that all employees are welcome to attend and most teams coordinate onsite team meetings around those events. We have at least one virtual event a quarter (Valentine's Day jeopardy, charity auction, etc.) as well. We also have impromptu monthly "watercooler" events where we spring an invite on employees on a*

*random Friday morning and have a discussion about
a relevant topic over coffee, just like you would
have done by a real watercooler. We also have free
lunches two times a month because free food is a
magical motivator.[29]*

Third, in deciding which events could be virtual and which should be in person, Michelich thought about some of the best parts of Jellyvision's culture and how to bring them to life through these different types of meetings.

Michelich thoughtfully shared with me:

*Let's be serious, we all stare at computers enough, so
it has to be **worth it** to participate. The virtual events
that really work are the ones that have a screen
component anyway. For example, we have a charity
auction every December (it's my favorite event of
the year) where Jellyvision employees auction off
goods or services to other employees for charity. The
auction takes place entirely on Slack and we have
slides that the auctioneers go through to explain
each item. It works great virtually because everyone
can participate equally, no matter their location.[30]*

But, Mustache Day, a ritual I wrote about in *Rituals Roadmap*, is a not-to-be-missed, in-person event that celebrates CEO Amanda Lannert's birthday. The ritual started back in 2007, when Harry Nathan Gottlieb, the founder of Jellyvision, along with Allard Laban, the chief creative officer, decided to turn the tables on Lannert, their then-president. Lannert would celebrate everyone else's birthday, but never her own. So, Gottlieb and Laban suggested that the employees come together to celebrate Lannert. As part of the celebration, a number of employees decided to grow out their mustaches and Mustache Day (a.k.a. Lannert's birthday) was born. And, over the past three years as new employees have joined Jellyvision, they've heard about this tradition. Employees can now come together in person again, and those new employees are excited to experience it firsthand.

When I asked Michelich how the feedback has been, she responded:

> *Overall, the feedback has been positive. Everything is optional, so people don't have to participate if they don't want to. In the end, people know that we are trying, which is a huge part of the battle. As long as we keep experimenting, people will keep trying it all out with us.*[31]

By giving Michelich and her team ownership and responsibility to curate and experiment with connections in person and virtually, Jellyvision isn't leaving fun to chance.

Hanging Out and Meeting Up

Meetup, the successful platform devoted to helping people find others with similar interests (both in person and online) knows a thing or two about the importance of connection. Which is why in June 2022, they hired Olga Ramesh as their people coordinator to ensure their 85-person, semi-remote team connected IRL. And connect they have! From bowling, to hidden talent presentations, to local hangouts, these (please note!) *during work hours* opportunities have been a big hit. The first of the local gatherings was in Queens and, according to Ramesh, "everything went well . . . beyond my expectations."[32]

It started with people connecting on Slack. They decided to meet in Astoria Park. Then, they all decided on food. People started chiming in about bringing blankets, beer, and snacks. When they met up, they found a shady spot and soon discovered connections outside of work, like the fact that some of the employees' kids attend the same school. They were "just a group of friends and not really talking about work," which from a business angle is pure gold.[33] All told, nine people showed up for this first hangout, including David Siegel, the CEO, who just happened to live close by.

Meeting up with real presence is serious business.

Gather@Greenhouse

Donald Knight, chief people officer of the 1,000-person software company Greenhouse, shared with me that, "Greenhouse wanted to be very intentional about prioritizing how to bring people together, so we built an employee experience team." Unfortunately, some of their offices have had to close, but Knight still believes "it is important to drive connection and proximity between people."[34]

Which is why they hired Rachel Allred for the employee experience team.

"What Allred focuses on every day is how do you curate the environment in which people can experience Greenhouse," Knight told me. And that environment includes more than just their physical offices and coworking spaces. "[Recently] that environment in San Francisco was in a bowling alley and we had about 50 people (we call 'Greenies') . . . do what we call 'Gather@.' "[35]

Gather@s are regular meetups (one or two times per month) that happen wherever clusters of Greenhouse talent live and work. So far, Gather@s have included Gather@ Boston, Gather@Austin, Gather@Atlanta, Gather@San Francisco, and Gather@Dublin. Allred is responsible for scouting locations, say a brewery or a winery, where Greenies can just be together for a couple hours—on purpose.

Gather@s are designed around a framework of the four stages of allyship (a.k.a. *IDEA*: inclusion, diversity, equity, allyship).[36] Or, as Knight calls it, the "maturity model of allyship." Nia Darville, senior manager of IDEA activations at Greenhouse, facilitates connection at these gatherings through ritualized activities, like the game We're Not Really Strangers. Greenies play this social game to help them get closer to each other. They answer questions like, "Do you think I was popular in high school? Why or why not?" and "Do you think I'm an early bird or a night owl?" and "On a scale from 1–10, how messy do you think my car is?" based solely on their perception of the person. Then, the person answers it and either validates or disproves other people's perceptions. As the game progresses, the questions get more personal (e.g., "What's your mom's name and what do you love most about her?" and "Describe your earliest happy memory." and "Tell me about the last time you cried.") and people can answer as vulnerably or as lightly as they want. As the facilitator, Darville tries to opt in to as much vulnerability as she can because "vulnerability begets vulnerability."[37]

Playing this game and other activities like it gives this distributed team the chance to gather and connect in person, share what matters to them and the experiences that have shaped them, and get to know the "soul behind Slack." Gather@s are truly a marriage between inclusion and connection. And, they are good for business. Darville shared with me, "in the beginning of a Gather@ we ask participants on a scale of 1–10, how connected do you feel to the other people in this room, and how connected do you feel to Greenhouse? After the event, we ask the question again and we see an average of a 32 percent increase in connection to Greenhouse and a 108 percent increase in connection to each other."[38]

We know good things happen when people connect. But, wow! Imagine the impact that that kind of connection has on your teams—especially if they are working hybrid or remote.

While Gather@ events are held in person, you can also have someone curate connections virtually.

Or can you?

Neiman Marcus Group's Variety Show Meetings

I want to attend a 90-minute, all-virtual meeting every month to hear company and team updates.

Said no one ever!

But then, how does Eric Severson, chief people and belonging officer for Neiman Marcus Group, get 90 to 100 percent of his 170-person people team to show up online month after month? Instead of a boring old meeting, NMG's people operations team puts on a veritable variety show!

First, a specific team hosts the meeting, so one month it could be recruiting, the next talent development, then business partners, and so on. And, there's an emcee (or two)—a virtual cruise director.

Second, there is a meeting template, which toggles between business updates, history quizzes (with prizes for winners), interviews with senior leaders, time to welcome new hires, and lots of celebrations, all of which "offer a very present, very ritualized experience."[39]

Third, a host from the team leading the meeting manages all the amazing tech to engage participants, from chats to emojis to polls to contests, so the meeting is more like a game show than a predictable meeting. As Erin Robertson, director of people strategy and analytics, shared with me:

> *There is almost a whole other meeting happening simultaneously in the chat. The 100-plus chat comments and countless emojis not only add clarity and additional context to the main content on screen, but show support, recognition, and build community among the remote teams. The support, the shout-outs, and the side conversations keep the meeting engaging and fun, and they continue even a day or two after the meeting.[40]*

Yes, it takes work and intention to make these meetings great. But the good news is that because the teams rotate hosting, when it's not your turn, you can sit back and enjoy the show.

Severson agreed. "The meeting is so engaging for everybody. You cannot just sit in the meeting. You're always asked to participate in different ways."[41]

And variety is the spice of flexible life.

Dropping in (in Person) at Dropbox

When Dropbox shifted to an asynchronous, virtual-first model during the pandemic, they faced "one of the highest attrition rates the company had ever experienced." Why? Some employees still preferred the nine-to-five schedule and, importantly, they "lost that in-person connection, which is required for shared identity and purpose."[42]

So what did they do?

Dropbox repurposed their offices into what they call "Dropbox Studios." It has all the amenities of a traditional office except for one notable exception—no space for individual work. The idea is that employees will gather in person for collaborative work and use the flexible spaces to meet their teams' needs. They also use these spaces—some permanent, some "on demand"—for quarterly off-sites. As they've decreased their real estate holdings, they've increased the budget for travel to enable everyone to attend these off-sites.

Please note: this shift is something lots of smart companies are doing.

Eager to cultivate another way to increase in-person connection, Dropbox created "Dropbox Neighborhoods" with "dedicated Slack channels for employees living in the same area to plan events like happy hours or volunteering days."[43] Neighborhoods give employees additional opportunities for social interaction with their colleagues—one aspect that was missing from their virtual-first work model.

To keep everyone connecting intentionally, each neighborhood is assigned a community manager to supervise planning. Some of the events put on by Neighborhoods have included "a virtual Halloween costume contest, a restaurant gift card raffle for Latinx Heritage Month, and a volunteer day at the San Francisco-Marin Food Bank for Bay area employees."[44] With 32 Neighborhoods, Dropbox is able to keep everyone connected.

What's been the response?

Not only has Dropbox seen a reduction in turnover and a 12 percent increase in employee engagement scores, but job seekers are noticing and want in on the fun. "Ninety percent of applicants cite Dropbox's location-agnostic policy as a reason to join the company."[45]

Adobe Designs Space for Dynamic Collaboration

When Adobe started building their Founders Tower back in 2018, they, of course, had no idea of the pandemic to come. Luckily, they didn't have to make too many adjustments to their office building design because they were "already working on spaces to accommodate distributed teams collaborating on creative projects. It's a software company for creatives, after all."[46] The future of work is baked right into this new construction: "sustainably built and run, optimized for hybrid, designed for community, adaptable, and resilient to change."

So, what does that look like?

It means these creatives will have more than "400 environments including team neighborhoods, focus rooms, collaboration zones, drop-in desks, adventure rooms, and community gathering grounds, along with the technology to support them."[47] Wow! I love how intentional Adobe is with this new space—they tailored it to both their employees' need for connection *and* their business needs.

They even go as far as to incorporate color psychology into their meeting spaces (which makes sense, as Adobe makes software for visual creatives). Different colors represent different optimal uses of spaces: "blue denotes focus, green promotes collaboration, and orange encourages connection and community."[48]

None of this was left to chance (or even creative whimsy). They researched team dynamics and tested everything from audio/video setups and meeting behavior to furniture.[49] But my favorite part is how they made an off-site space on-site at the office. Teams or departments can "gather distributed employees into a physical space and host hackathons, annual kickoffs, and other forms of large team events in an area reminiscent of the conference accommodations of a hotel, but nicer. The vibes are split between elements of both work and play to accommodate all kinds of thinkers."[50]

Talk about designing a day in the office that's worth the commute.

Protocols

You've let go of the need to meet for the sake of meeting. You appreciate that presence is more than just being physically present. And you realize that meetings are not going away. Flexibility is not going away. The need for connection and belonging is not going away.

Whether your company is in person, remote, or somewhere in between, meetings play a critical role (even more so nowadays) in how people feel about work. How can your meetings maximize all of these different variables? It's not easy, and the rules keep changing in this Wild West of work today. So, what do we need in the Wild West? We need a sheriff to keep some order.

And guess what? You're it!

So, next, I'll share some nitty-gritty protocols from sheriffs just like you—people charged with keeping their meetings on track. As you consider ways to hold your meetings, keep in mind that you're also looking for approaches to capture and maintain people's attention for as long as you need it.

After all, according to a Doodle study, badly run meetings cost US companies nearly $400 billion each year in lost productivity. Respondents said that participating in poorly organized meetings led to not enough time to do the rest of their work, unclear actions and confusion, loss of focus on projects, and irrelevant attendees slowing progress.[51]

Here are seven basic rules to help you sheriffs meet as you mean to go on:

1. **Establish a meeting strategy and cadence.** Weekly, quarterly, and yearly gatherings are more important than ever to keep people connected to each other and the company. As Jaleh Rezaei, cofounder and CEO of Mutiny, wrote on Twitter, "We needed a new rhythm. One that generated the same amount of cumulative connection and context, but relied on less frequent in-person time. In other words—one BIG quarterly wave to replace lots of tiny daily waves."[52] No meeting should be an island. At Greenhouse, the HR leadership team has quarterly off-sites. Each one is 72 hours and focuses on a theme—Q1: talent, Q2: long-term planning, Q3: short-term planning, and Q4: budget.

2. **Assign a host to curate connection.** Even if you don't hire someone to take care of all your gatherings, you will want to tap someone from your team to maintain your protocols, whatever you decide they should be. Using

their employee experience experimentation engine, Lab82, Adobe tested a hybrid off-site meeting and found that assigning a meeting facilitator helped keep everyone on track and "drove team-building activities, like icebreakers, food experiences, and wellbeing stretch breaks" to provide belonging, trust, and engagement.[53] Whether in person or virtual, all employees joined the meeting from their laptops and used the chat feature to have group discussions (instead of in-person conversation). Lunch was catered for the in-person participants, and gift cards or vouchers were provided to those who joined virtually. These best practices helped facilitate inclusion. Or, go one step further—gathering expert Priya Parker suggests having both an in-person *and* a virtual host for hybrid meetings.

3. **Start as you mean to go on.** Eileen Fisher, a leading women's fashion brand, opens their meetings by ringing an actual chime, indicating that it's time for a centering moment of quiet. Microsoft CEO Satya Nadella opens his senior leadership meeting with what he calls "Researcher of the Amazing," where an executive shares a story about how Microsoft technology is being used to make a difference in the world. Storytelling is a great way to grab people's attention and keep them engaged. Company rituals are a great place to start.

4. **Take the pledge.** In response to the challenges of attending so many meetings, and with the increase in working from home, the CEO of IBM created a pledge.[54] I love their pledge, but we should all create our own. And stick to it! Here are some highlights from IBM's:

   • I pledge to set boundaries and prevent video fatigue.

- I will use new time limit boundaries for meetings, recognizing video fatigue is real and a new phenomenon for all of us.
- I will shift to 20- and 45-minute meetings to replace our normal 30-minute and 1-hour calls as much as possible.
- I will avoid setting up any full-day or half-day meetings. If a long meeting is required, I will ensure we take short breaks every hour, that no session is longer than two hours, and every two hours there is a 30-minute break.

5. **Mind your manners.** Start and end on time (or even early!), stick to the agenda (and send it out beforehand), and only invite people who need to be there. Fully-remote software company Zapier uses automation to make sure everyone's time is used wisely. As Brandon Sammut, chief people officer, told CNBC, "We have automations that create an agenda, send it to participants ahead of time to complete and review, and send people a Zoom link ahead of the meeting. Automation makes us more productive during our meetings, so we can focus on discussing ideas rather than inputting and reviewing updates."[55]

6. **Find the sweet spot between tech and connect.** Leverage tech and all its benefits. These days, there are so many options, from breakout rooms to virtual hand raising, to polls, to pairing people up, to small group breakouts. And as AI continues to develop and advance, companies have started using it to make meetings more efficient. Sembly AI, a company formed by former C-suite officers at EY and Visual Trading Systems, "leverages the power

of AI to pull out the moments that matter."[56] Using AI tools to transcribe or summarize key information gives the humans in the room more time for innovation and collaboration. And as nascent as this tech is, it's already making a difference. A study of three companies using this kind of AI found that "virtual meeting efficiency improved by 25%."[57]

7. **Experiment, experiment, experiment.** Leaders, we have never been through times like these. The pendulum will continue to swing. As you roll out protocols, remind your employees (and yourself) to proceed with empathy and experimentation. Things will likely change again. Start with small groups, iterate, assess, and see what works. Change course if need be.

A recent survey found that most people would rather go to the dentist than attend a "bad meeting."[58] (Clearly, I love stats that compare bad business practices to dental upkeep!) They'd also rather talk politics at a family dinner!

I don't blame them. But meetings don't have to be grueling and painful. There are options. Lots of them—just like jobs for your most talented employees.

With the rising tide in time we all spend on our screens, it's critical to be judicious whenever we ask people to step away from their thinking work to attend a meeting, even if it's in person.

Once you learn how to pick and choose wisely—with purpose, presence, and protocols—you'll learn how to meet as you'd like to go on, and on, and on.

That's a (W)RAP

Retention Action Plan for Meetings

1. Challenge yourself to list all your meetings and see if you can state the purpose for each. If there is no purpose, there should be no meeting. Often, a simple email or Slack message providing an update can suffice.

2. Prioritize presence—both physical and psychological— whether you are gathering IRL or virtually. Always remember that there is a human being on the other side of that table or screen. Do your best to give them your full attention. By the way, this is much easier if you've gotten rid of all of your meetings that were not purposeful (see Number One above).

3. When in doubt, leave them out. Sorry! But when your invitations are limited to those who *really, really* need to be there, you're sending the message that you value everyone's time. Meetings that are focused and smaller tend to be more successful.

4. Create a connection curator role to make sure people are actually connecting with each other, especially in environments that are hybrid or remote. The reality is, left to our own devices, real connections can be tricky! So, make it part of someone's job—or even create a new position to facilitate connections.

5. Establish meeting protocols or rules of the road that align with your company culture. Be intentional. Determine meeting cadences, critical attendees, who will host, how you should start and end a meeting, meeting timelines, and how to stick to these best practices. The best protocols often become rituals.

CHAPTER FIVE

FROM LADDERS TO LILY PADS

Learning and Development for the Human Professional

OLD IDEA #5

Professional development should be job-related.

NEW BEGINNING #5

Taking professional development personally is fuel for the ecosystem of opportunity.

art Lindsley was the head of global process excellence for people operations at Google—what a title, huh?—and is now their strategic advisor of people experience. He's a writer and professor, and he's been in the HR space for a long time. These days, he refers to himself as a "business architect," which is how every leader ought to think of themselves as they build and rebuild companies for the employees of today.

In 2021, Lindsley wrote something that I think is critical to consider as we design the future of business: "Employees are not inputs to production, not bought things, not assets or capital: they're *customers*."[1]

Indeed. In the Retention Revolution, employees *are* the new customers. And while these new customers may not always be right, I've found that one of the biggest requests of employees today is actually very good for business.

And that's professional development—lots of it, right off the bat, with no strings attached.

Now, before you try to imagine how to offer an array of expensive conferences, lunch and learns, and skills training to all your brand-new employees—and expect nothing in return—rest assured, today's professional development is something else entirely.

Of course, there's still room and a need for traditional professional development, but the big difference in today's workplace is that it's not led solely by the employers' needs, but by the employees'—the *customers'*—interests as well. So much so that it doesn't even necessarily have anything to do with their day job. Even so, it should happen during the workday.

So, what do you get out of it?

Well, not what you think.

Professional development in the Retention Revolution is not the quid pro quo of before times, the old "I pay you to learn something and you apply your skills to my enterprise" arrangement. Today, it's more like "let's work together to make sure everyone grows."

End of story.

In Steve Cadigan's book *Workquake*, he rounds up leaders' thoughts on this new take on professional development. This desire for experience, for growth, for learning is the fuel behind what Kevin Lyman, an HR executive with 30 years of global experience, calls "talent velocity,"[2] an idea at the heart of the Retention Revolution. Or as Daniel Ek, the founder and CEO of Spotify, puts it: "You have a number of years [or months!] when you perform a job, and then your tour is over, and it's time for you to think about what the next step is."[3]

But wait, why on earth would we want to accept and support that people are thinking about their next step?

Because they are.

And when you get ahead of the curve—people *are* going to leave—and participate in the process instead of keeping it shrouded in secrecy, all parties involved have the potential to grow together in new ways. And who knows? Maybe the employee will discover that the thing they're looking for is where they've always been.

Here's a great illustration: at the 2022 Wharton Leadership Conference (aptly named "The End of the Beginning"), SHRM CEO Johnny C. Taylor Jr. talked about the changing nature of employee tenure. Employees used to stay for a certain amount of time *after* their company paid for them to get a degree or develop in some way. The difference, Taylor said, is that now employees don't feel obligated to stay. Instead, they will say, "The reason I stayed the last three years was because you were paying for my degree!"[4]

This is a big shift in the employee/employer contract. It's the difference between *having* to stick around and *wanting* to stick around. I mean, you're all for supporting employees, customers, . . . *people!* You want to do the right thing. And, of course, you want people to have meaning in their lives and you love the idea of playing any part in adding purpose to people's jobs.

But—you're running a business here. How can you justify footing the bill for your employees' learning and development, which might develop them right out the door? Well, remember the revolving door of opportunity I discussed in the Introduction? Remember the irony of "if you love them, let them leave"? Well, in this case, if you love them, let them learn.

Because that's what people really, really want. And in the Retention Revolution, your job as a leader is to constellate your business goals and values around serving your market and all of your customers, including your employees.

So, please allow me to build the business case for taking professional development very personally, with no strings attached, from the very beginning of an employee's tenure. As Lindsley puts it, "When we see that employees are customers . . . business is transformed. And the opportunity is enormous."[5]

The Business Case

Of everything I've researched for the Retention Revolution, the case for taking professional development personally is remarkably clear and accessible. The numbers speak for themselves.

A June 2021 Gartner study found that "only 33% of candidates who sought out a new job in the past 12 months searched internally within their organization first."[6] But a lack of development opportunities is often cited as one of the top reasons people leave their companies in the first place.

So, why wouldn't current employees look to their companies first?

For starters, a majority of employees don't even realize there *are* opportunities in the first place. In the same study, Gartner found that "only 51% of candidates report that they are aware of internal job openings available at their organization,"[7] and the iCIMS 2023 Workforce Report noted that "58% of people find it difficult to find open jobs to apply for at their company."[8]

This is a huge opportunity for leaders lying in plain sight. If you can create awareness, access, and support for internal mobility and career progression, you can retain and grow your top talent. A 2015 Deloitte survey found that for employees in a strong learning culture, "engagement and retention rates are also 30–50% higher."[9]

And, it doesn't have to break the bank.

As Taylor Blake, SVP Product for Degreed Academies and Benefits, put it so well, not only is development now the expectation—not the exception—but "upskilling employees is cheaper than rehiring them."[10] Plus, economic downturns don't last forever, so if you continue upskilling employees when other companies have scaled back learning and development, you'll have a competitive edge.

Looking through the DEI lens makes professional development an even bigger win. One 2022 study from Terawatt, a group coaching platform, discovered that underrepresented groups were less satisfied with professional development.[11] A *Harvard Business Review* study found that offering professional development opportunities is key in attracting and retaining employees of color.[12] Finally, the think tank Conference Board found that in 2022, "most employees highly value the opportunity to develop work-related skills." And yet, "Despite the high value placed on professional development opportunities, people of color report a greater lack of access to these opportunities and resources."[13]

If you're serious about creating a culture that invites and supports a diverse range of talent, then professional development—the kind that's accessible to *all*—is the way to go.

Hopefully I've made my case for professional development. So, the question becomes how?

How can you integrate professional development into your employee experience in such a way that's personal to them *and* impactful to you and your company?

A 2021 McKinsey study described it well: "It is a profound reorientation away from a traditional top-down model." What exactly does this mean? It means making revolutionary shifts in the way you think about how people's individual growth can fuel your business. "This shift allows a company to put its workers first by exploring and responding to how they view their employee journeys, then delivering tailored interventions that focus on critical moments that matter to maximize satisfaction, performance, and productivity."[14]

The following are case studies from companies that are rethinking professional development: early and often; up, down, and sideways; and from the inside out. As you read these inspiring stories, consider all the opportunities that already exist in your company for cross-fertilization and how you might experiment with your teams. Remember, all the people who you're about to meet are human, just like you. Everyone had to start somewhere.

Early and Often
(With No Strings Attached)

As you know from Chapter One, starting as you mean to go on is the best way to create a meaningful culture, which includes a learning culture. After all, when else will you have such a captive audience?

And with everything we do in the human workplace, designing your professional development to complement your values is the most efficient and effective way to educate your employees, not only about the content of your offerings, but also about their new community.

Chipotle Schools Us All

The rockstar of early and often, no strings attached professional development is Chipotle, the company whose revenue was up 17 percent in 2022, compared with the 10 percent average of similar restaurants.[15] I say that just to prepare you for the unbelievable professional development they offer, lest you think they're going out of business as a result.

They most definitely are not.

OK, for starters, they offer *free* college education in a variety of fields, and a stipend of more than $5,000 for a wider range of programs—all with no strings. While most Chipotle benefits start after 30 days, full college reimbursement (understandably) kicks in after four months of working a minimum of 15 hours per week. After that time, crew members can get a four-year degree with one of the accredited universities or colleges in their consortium and be absolutely debt free by graduation.

Does that mean that someone could get a four-year degree paid for by Chipotle and then walk away?

It sure does.

Chipotle also offers free therapy, free career certificates, *and* free meals.

So, I asked Daniel Banks, director of global benefits, how can they justify this kind of spending on an individual's development without a clear and obvious payback?

His answer was simple: "We recognize that the people are the lifeblood of our organization."[16]

Easy to say, but it's only when you truly understand the ecosystem of opportunity that you will be able to create programs with this much confidence.

Banks continued:

> *We actually see that in our retention statistics where people who engage in [the college reimbursement] program, they want to stick around. . . . In 2021, we promoted 90% of our restaurant managers from internal promotions, including 79% of our general managers. So we know that there's a real robust pipeline of*

individuals and talents that we are cultivating to be our future leaders. So it's a win-win situation.[17]

The fact of the matter is taking care of the people in your company is good for business. Banks is absolutely right when he says, "If someone were to leave the organization, generally speaking, they're going to have a positive reaction to our brand, and they're going to be an external brand ambassador who wants to come back, wants to enjoy the food . . . it's all about our culture, our mission, and our values."[18]

That is *exactly* what the Retention Revolution is all about.

52+ Hours of Learning at Rackspace

Rackspace Technology is a global company with 6,000 people on four continents. In order to ensure their employees have equal access to development opportunities, they offer all their employees a program called 52+ Learning Hours. The initiative includes technical certification programs (most at no cost to Rackers) and learning and development opportunities (with the support of their premier partners like Amazon, Google, and Microsoft). "We're fueling a culture of continuous development and creating excitement around learning,"[19] said RaChelle Streetman, director of global talent development. They also offer an innovative leadership program (ILP), as well as many other opportunities "for Rackers to plug in and sharpen their skill sets," as PJ Lovejoy, senior manager, Racker experience and HR communications, told me. And my favorite part of this extensive initiative is that, as Lovejoy shared, "We really lean into our core value of Expertise, as we know that our Racker Expertise helps shape Racker careers and ultimately powers our customers' success."[20]

Which is just the point—early and often growth (based on your values) for growth's sake will create an ecosystem of opportunity, which helps everyone thrive.

At O.C. Tanner, "If You're Interested, You're Invited"

O.C. Tanner, a 95-year-old employee experience company, knows a thing or two about employee appreciation. And part of that appreciation is letting employees and new hires know that they will have opportunities to grow at and with O.C. Tanner. As Mindi Cox, chief marketing and people officer, told Daniel and Stephen Huerta on the *Modern People Leader* podcast, "We need to grow [employees]. When someone shows up for an interview, we have to paint a picture of how they will grow with us, not how they will stay with us. . . . We have to grow as a company, and we have to know they are on board to grow with us."[21]

I had the chance to speak with Cox, and she expanded on how they bring this important point home early and often.

On day one, she meets with new hires and says, "Welcome to O.C. Tanner. Thank you for choosing us. We hope that you feel like that decision is reinforced every step of the way, especially on your first day," which is pretty standard onboarding fare. But then, she says:

> *Now, we've hired you in for a specific position—we would love for you to be committed and an expert at*

learning the position that you've been hired into. But if you become curious or feel like you want a mentor or need to learn the company in a different way, don't let that hold you back from raising your hand and asking for what you need.[22]

In other words, "if you're interested, you're invited."[23]

At O.C. Tanner, professional development is seen as a competitive advantage. By giving employees opportunities for lateral movement or promotions, the company helps them find not only the role where they're best suited to learn and grow, but also where they can best offer value, which is in the long-term interest of the company. Sometimes, that even means when a new employee is hired, if leadership realizes they're better suited for a different (or even higher up!) role, that employee will move into that position immediately.

Cox truly gets it.

Later in the *Modern People Leader* episode, she spelled out the three pieces of the self-determination theory (SDT), which says that at the root of our deepest happiness, we need to feel autonomy, mastery, and connectedness. "The workplace is so uniquely situated to offer all three of those things every single day. . . . Competence, right? Mastery. Can I help grow you to the point where you feel like, on most days, 'I nailed that. I'm an expert at that.' "[24] Which is why at O.C. Tanner, a discussion about growth is baked right into the employee experience—from day one. And if you're thinking, *That all sounds good, but what's the point?* Their strategy is clearly working—Cox reported on the same podcast that they've been shattering revenue goals with more than 20 percent growth in the past two years alone.

THE **SWEET SPOT**
BETWEEN **TECH & CONNECT**

GLOAT

Gloat is a workforce agility platform that powers internal talent marketplaces for some of the biggest companies in the world. A talent marketplace identifies the skills and aspirations of employees and matches them with projects and opportunities across the organization. Sounds simple, but not so much!

Ben Reuveni, cofounder and CEO, came up with the idea for Gloat when he felt firsthand how the silos of a large company could limit a person's potential. After serving as team leader in an elite technological intelligence unit (8200) in the Israeli Defense Forces, Reuveni joined a startup that was acquired by IBM. As he tried to pursue opportunities within the company, he realized that it was easier for him to find roles *outside* of the company than within it.

That's when he thought, *This shouldn't be so difficult.*

> I was working at an organization with thousands of jobs and had skills that would allow me to contribute so much more than my role allowed, but there was no way for me to find new, exciting work that leveraged my full capabilities. I knew countless others felt as stuck as I did. So I felt obligated to do something about it.[25]

So, he started Gloat—a tech platform that uncovers the full skill sets and aspirations of employees, gives employees control over their careers, and helps businesses redeploy and develop talent at scale. Something they call "Workforce Agility."

Danny Shteinberg, Gloat cofounder and CMO, shared with me a perfect example of how Gloat partners with one of their clients, Unilever, to help employees find their sweet spot.

Vanessa Otake is an engineer by training who worked in a technical research and development role at Unilever and is now in an HR role in the middle of her career. Looking to grow and learn on the job, Otake checked out Unilever's flex work program (powered by Gloat) and decided to take on a diversity and inclusion project while still in her current job. The project energized her and got her creative juices flowing. She learned something new and brought a new perspective to the team. And when a full-time role opened up on the HR team, she had the experience and the relationships to get the position and hit the ground running. A win-win—for her and Unilever!

As Otake shared with *Business Insider*, "I'm back into learning again, growing again, and being able to grow with something that I'm really passionate about."[26] In fact, "Now that I'm in this role, I feel like a kid in a sweet shop," she said.

Up, Down, and Sideways

Gone are the days when professional development was a one-and-done conference, webinar, or online class. And at smart companies, you no longer need to search outside of your organization for opportunities. Some of the most exciting professional development is happening *inside* companies through mentoring, sponsorship, shadowing, internal internships, recruitment strategies, and being creative about roles. For instance, Chipotle, in addition to their incredible support for professional development, is committed to hiring from within to meet the ongoing demand for talent. According to an article in *Fortune*, "In 2022, Chipotle says, it had approximately 22,000 internal promotions, including all of its U.S. regional vice president openings, 81% of team directors, and 74% of field leader positions."[27]

Wise of Chipotle to do so—because it's a great way to keep people connected to your company. As LinkedIn CEO Ryan Roslansky shared in *Fortune*:

> *If you understand the skills of your existing workforce, and where you need to go as a company, there's a huge opportunity to help your top talent find different roles inside of your company instead of learning and leaving. In fact, our data shows that at the two-year mark, an employee who has made an internal move has a 75% likelihood of staying as opposed to the mere 56% likelihood for an employee that hasn't made an internal move.[28]*

When you let go of the traditional trajectories of advancement and old-school visions of a career path, you're free to swap and share positions and expertise. Employee learning shifts from predictable modules and programs to a more experimental approach. And people stay!

The fact is real ideation as opposed to just plug-and-play exercises is the kind of learning people want. And from a business perspective, it makes all the sense in the world. What better way to keep people connected and inspired than to help them learn from their colleagues and provide opportunities for them to develop within your own company? Helen Tupper and Sarah Ellis, authors of the bestselling book *The Squiggly Career: Ditch the Ladder, Discover Opportunity, Design Your Career,* refer to this trajectory as "squiggling."[29] Here are some case studies to help you see how to squiggle successfully.

The Internal-Ship at Citigroup and Real Chemistry

Laine Joelson Cohen, head of learning and development for human resources at the banking giant Citigroup, realized that the HR department was so busy making sure employees across the company had access to learning and development opportunities that HR was experiencing a bit of the "Cobbler's Children Syndrome." As in, the experts go without!

As Cohen put it, "Sometimes, we're doing this for the organization, and we weren't focusing on ourselves." She understands that "one of the big ways that people want to learn and that we know people learn well from experience is through stretch assignments, but . . . moving people across borders is really difficult to do."[30]

So, they created the "Experience Hub" where employees can essentially shop for new opportunities within the company. The Experience Hub works alongside their learning portal for HR employees to discover development opportunities within the company and move in any direction. To bring opportunities to the Hub, they solicited projects from HR managers that employees can apply to participate in. The main goal of these three–five hours per week stretch assignments is to help employees "grow their network, grow their skills, and build their résumés" without ever having to leave the company.

Real Chemistry is one of those very cool digital, global, creative companies that's pulling out all the stops to create a better user experience—in their case, in healthcare. And they're crushing it—for the last reported quarter in 2022, their growth was 21 percent.[31]

In 2022, the company took an unusual step, which is now being imitated by others, by creating a role for someone to lead communications, culture, and purpose. The forward-thinking approach of putting what many have historically considered "softer" skills into the C-suite was a sign that the organization was thinking differently about its people.

Wendy Carhart, Real Chemistry's first chief communications, culture, and purpose officer, knew that being intentional was what would keep the culture alive when everyone was working in a Zoom box: "Real Chemistry has gone through tons of acquisitions. And so, the good news about that is it provides lots of opportunities for people to learn new things and take on different challenges."[32] Being both remote and hybrid *and* a company with different groups, teams, and companies created significant challenges for building a collaborative and connected culture. Carhart's charge was to find ways to bring people together, drive the business forward, and build a new culture—one that meets the needs of all employees regardless of where they sit in the world or the organization.

But this only works with intention.

Carhart introduced me to Jennifer Paganelli (a.k.a. Jpags), president of earned media and integration, to learn more about how she helps bring one of the key tenets of the company—always evolving—to life. Paganelli shared that their exit interview data showed that employees wanted to gain more skills in other parts of the organization, and they were leaving to get that experience. She told me, "If people are excellent and motivated, committed and curious, why the heck wouldn't we want to keep them here?"[33]

A great question.

In response, Real Chemistry launched their "Hybrid Program" so that people could learn across the organization. Employees in the program spend 50 percent of their time on their "old jobs" and 50 percent on developing new skills. Real Chemistry took nominations for the program, and the response was overwhelming. In this lily pad model of professional development, selected individuals get the opportunity to spend six weeks "hopping" over to a different department, checking out new things, and seeing what intrigues or excites them. With service offerings ranging from advertising and medical solutions to data, AI, and integrated marketing and communications, there are many places to leap.

Paganelli assumed the program would resonate primarily with younger employees, but people of all levels and ages threw their hats in the ring. The cohort ages spanned 20 years, proving the old adage false: you *can* teach an old dog new tricks. "People want to keep growing. They want to learn from each other. In this program, we are not just training someone on a new skill set but giving them an opportunity to partner with new people across their 'long hallway.' " The program's success can also be attributed to the number of people who got involved to make it happen and part of the DNA. "Mid-level managers who are hungry to pay it forward determine the curriculum, HR meets with hybrids to check in and provide support, senior leaders speak to the group, and every cohort participant becomes 'honorary members' of the teams they were hybridizing."[34]

It's a total intern(al)ship for the whole company!

While of course there's nothing wrong with wanting to advance from, say, manager to director, the point of the Real Chemistry Hybrid Program is "really to learn different skills that are going to, you know, saturate your curiosity."[35] And at the end of the program, employees get to decide whether they'd like to move to the new group or take their added skills back to their old group, which gives them a more holistic perspective on the work and the company.

No program is a guarantee that people will stay forever. But, after an experience like this, they'll tell all their friends, and the virtuous cycle will go on.

And on . . .

Out of the Shadows at GitLab

Remember GitLab, the biggest all-remote company in the world? Well, they also have an incredible remote mentorship program, which includes opportunities for junior employees, minorities in tech, and women at GitLab.

My favorite GitLab offering, though, is their CEO Shadow program, which is, ironically, done in person (when possible). Anyone in the company can apply to shadow the CEO for two weeks, which includes traveling with the CEO, attending almost all of his meetings, and participating in short-term work. Takeaways from a manager's point of view include confidence building, better judgment, and a more thorough understanding of the company's values. And, of course, since the CEO has a hand in so many of the different teams and functions within the company, this shadowing opportunity is a way to understand the inner workings of the entire organization and an incredible way to learn how to "manage up."[36]

The shadow's next move may not be an obvious one, as in inching toward "the top," but by the time they're ready to make a change, they'll have exposure to senior leadership and will be a whole lot more connected to the company, regardless of how long they stay.

Developing Out the Side Door at Comcast and American Eagle Outfitters

Cherie Arabia is a leader at Comcast who is committed to helping her direct reports find the right role, even if it means directing them away from her team or from Comcast altogether. Arabia described two employees on her team who wanted growth and a promotion; unfortunately, there weren't any such opportunities available on her team, so "we agreed that we would search for opportunities together and meet regularly to discuss options."[37]

Arabia invested in sending one employee to a training program to expand his skill set, and she found several gig assignments for the other employee to gain exposure to—and experience with—other areas of the business. And yes, all this was in addition to their day jobs—professional development in the Retention Revolution is a two-way street!

So, I asked Arabia the million-dollar question: Did her efforts to help her employees develop outside of her team encourage these employees to stay, if not on her team, then at least in the company?

Yes. As Arabia shared, "Each [employee] ended up finding incredible internal positions. They had tremendous
gratitude for the support, new interesting growth opportunities, and the understanding that Comcast is a company that
develops and invests in their people."[38]

Up, down, and sideways.

When I asked her how she felt about that, she told me
everything you need to know about why it's so important to
rethink professional development to include the side door:

> *I was delighted for them. I've never hoarded talent
> because I think all it does is build resentment. It
> builds resentment for the organization and distrust
> for you as a leader and a person. Confident leaders
> know the value of growing talent. I now have
> employee friends and internal allies in different
> organizations within the company. Each left my team
> with pride and an experience where they knew they
> were valued. We celebrated each of them on their
> exits and shared their stories with the whole team.
> They may come back to my team or to a different part
> of the organization or they may leave permanently.
> It's important to understand their impact, promote
> their contributions, and acknowledge their grit
> and effort required to seek the best opportunities
> for themselves and the company. . . . It's a win for
> them personally. It's a win for me as a leader. And
> ultimately a win for the company.[39]*

Speaking of the side door . . .

Nathan Jun Poekert is the head of social and content
at American Eagle Outfitters. In October 2022, he wrote a
moving LinkedIn post[40] paying homage to one of his direct

reports who left American Eagle to pursue her dream of becoming a sommelier.

The story, as he tells it, is that his top-performing employee, Eun, "expressed a certain level of professional exhaustion. She was doing her job (very well I might add) and was on track for career advancement at AE but expressed that she no longer felt inspired creatively and was considering what she wanted to do with her career path."

Turns out, her dream was to become a certified sommelier.

Eun soon made a bold request: "She told me she would need to leave work early 3 days a week to start taking classes to be a certified sommelier. Of course I approved and even was excited for her. A few months after that she requested to relocate to Spain for a month to experience wine culture there. Again I approved."

Cut to: "The day she told me she got a full-time job offer to be a sommelier in a NYC restaurant I only had excitement for her. I am, of course, sad to see someone I've spent almost eight years of my professional life with leave . . . but as a manager, there's no prouder feeling than seeing someone you mentored, trained, and managed accomplish and reach a dream."

As Jun Poekert tells every person that works for him, "My job as your manager isn't to get you to perform your best here. My job is to prepare you for your next job." And sometimes that means helping them prepare to switch careers.

It takes a pretty gracious human to say goodbye to an employee you truly value, even the ones you helped "reach a dream." But even if you develop an employee right out the door, they will always feel connected to the boss who helped make it happen. This is the revolutionary spirit that keeps the ecosystem of opportunity in motion.

Hopefully by now, you can see how to develop employees up through mentoring and sideways through opportunities across the organization.

But down?

How can professional development work . . . downward?

And no, I'm not talking about opting out or quitting (quietly or otherwise), or signing off for greener pastures. Though in Chapter Seven, we'll meet some folks who decided to return to their jobs for various reasons—the boomerangs.

What we're talking about here is being strategic and moving—up, down, and sideways—around an organization so that everybody learns what they need and how to get it.

So, how does it work?

Just ask Debbie Lovich, a senior partner at Boston Consulting Group, who prides herself on being "the fastest employee promoted to partner at BCG and the slowest to senior partner ever."

Which is to say, when Lovich's four kids hit middle school, she resigned as partner so she could be home more often for her family. But, because BCG was smart, they suggested that Lovich give up her long-distance clients instead, and help develop local businesses, which she did for a couple of years. Then, as she shared with me, "When that didn't provide enough balance, I resigned as a partner and moved to an internal role . . . I was basically the COO of the Boston office and took on global and regional efforts to improve how we work/operate."[41]

Now, as senior partner, Lovich is in a position to ensure that more employees have the kind of professional development opportunity she had. She told me, "So you've got this mix of people who are recalibrating in their own life. Companies need to really up their game around how to build a relationship with an employee, because otherwise we won't have loyalty. How do you deliver that? What does it take?"[42]

For one thing, it takes the willingness to think outside the box about professional development—for both the company and the employee. Think about roles that might have worked better for you at a certain time in your career, but you didn't want to ask. Thinking creatively about internal mobility, up, sideways, and even downward, can create generations of leaders who can change the culture of a company forever.

Inside Out

OK, so there are lots of ways to grow up, down, and sideways. Check. But what does it mean to develop professionally from the inside out?

In many ways, this is really the heart of professional development in the Retention Revolution—literally, as the very best professional development connects with people's hearts. And the stats reflect this. Deloitte found that in companies with a robust learning culture "engagement and retention rates are 30–50 percent higher."[43]

And yes, these kinds of opportunities ideally should happen on the clock. Because taking professional development personally is not just good for people; it's great for business.

Let's take a look at some companies who get this right.

Invest in Yourself at InDay

LinkedIn, which has one of the most impactful professional development programs out there with the most regular cadence, also gives employees the opportunity to learn in ways that work for them. InDay is their monthly "Investment Day," a day set aside for employees to focus on "themselves, the company, and the world."[44]

I attended a wellness-themed InDay while doing research for my second book. Between morning meditation class, a country line dancing class, and a wellness fair, it was impossible not to take professional development very personally.

What makes InDay so personal is that employees are encouraged to participate in whatever ways work best for them. So, while there is on-site programming offered through the day, employees can invest in themselves however they like. At the wellness InDay I attended, one of the employees was in her exercise clothes. As I recall in *Rituals Roadmap*, "she had decided to jog to work, check out the InDay offerings, do a little work, and then jog home. That was her personal, wellness-inspired InDay."[45] For the creativity InDay that year, one employee stayed home and used the time to paint her daughter's bedroom in a unicorn theme.[46]

One of the things that makes InDay so impactful is that it happens all day *during work hours*. This is another very important aspect of great professional development to remember. In the before times, companies could afford to throw people a professional development bone (not that it was smart or effective!) and trust them to take care of it all on their own time. Well, today—as you know—with home and work time so blurred, such distinctions make less sense than ever. And managers know that unless something is "mission critical," employees are urged to take advantage of and experience the magic of InDay.

Next Up: Lattice Values

Lattice is a software company with products that "turn employees into high performers, managers into leaders, and companies into the best places to work." So it should come as no surprise that taking professional development personally is fundamental to their work.

The idea of development is even baked into one of the company's values, "What's Next?" This alludes to the fact that Lattice gives every employee (all levels and tenure) a $500 stipend that can be used to help them grow and develop however they want. The stipend doesn't need to tie directly to an employee's job, act as admission to a conference, or prove ROI. According to Alia Le Cam, global director of communications and public relations, at Lattice, "we are really intentional about letting the employee be in the driver's seat for those decisions. . . . If you are feeling fulfilled and you're challenging yourself, that will show up in some way in the work that you're doing and in the way that you're interacting with colleagues."[47]

Cara Allamano, Lattice's chief people officer, took this value to heart when she signed up for an "intense humanities class" at the University of Chicago. She explained, "I was doing it to get my brain into a totally different space, but what I realized was that when I came back to work, I was so fresh and gained the capability to see things differently. When I was asked, 'What would Aristotle say about this?' I actually had an opinion about it."[48]

Allamano went on to tell me about a colleague of hers who took an online improv class, because a girl he had dated said he wasn't funny enough. He's in sales, and he began to see how improv actually helped in his work. "This is when we talk about the whole person and partnering with our employees in a new way. . . . The companies that grab onto that and execute it—they will be the winners."[49]

It's not always clear from the outset how personal growth will impact a person's work, but because we're human, I guarantee it will.

The Power of Personal Connections

Taking professional development personally also means taking full advantage of the power of relationships and personal connections that naturally arise among people. You can do this in a variety of accessible ways.

One of the most popular methods for delivering professional development from the inside out is through coaching. In fact, one-on-one or cohort coaching is one of the most requested employee benefits and a perfect way for companies to help people take their own professional development personally, which is what employees want—sometimes even more than money.[50]

However, until recently, coaching was available mostly for the C-suite and other high performers whom a company deemed "worthy" of the often-significant investment. Over the past few years, and especially since the pandemic, managers and HR leaders have been so overwhelmed that they have turned more and more to coaching.

And it's a proven win for companies.[51]

One exciting development in the coaching world that lowers the financial stakes a bit is the trend toward increased access to employees at all levels. There's a whole new category of companies popping up that offer organizations coaching beyond the C-suite through a variety of means, such as AI or group coaching. Companies like Bravely, BetterUp, Torch, and Modern Health are all in the business of democratizing coaching so that more individual contributors can benefit, which, in turn, benefits the whole. As one Deloitte study notes, "A coaching culture is the practice that's most highly correlated with business performance, employee engagement, and overall retention."[52]

Another inspired way to bring the power of coaching to your employees, especially those who are underserved, is to curate connection in groups or cohorts. For instance, The Cru helps companies lift up what Tiffany Dufu, founder and CEO, calls "the woman in the middle"—geographically, professionally, and generationally—by connecting her with other like-minded women in a peer-led, intracompany accountability group.

Why would a company want to pay for its employees to connect with other employees? As Dufu put it so well:

What we're finding is that there are basically three things that this woman in the middle really desires, and if an employer can deliver them, they've got her hooked. The first is meaning. Everyone wants to live some kind of purposeful life and is on a quest to do that. And in as much as an employer can assign the purpose or help her to understand that in relationship to her role there, great. The second is advancement. Not just—I want to get a promotion, or I want more money. She wants evidence that she's a better person, and that she's really grown, that she's evolved. The third thing is integration and not

*just hybrid work flexibility. She wants to know that
her company values and acknowledges and is willing
to invest in the holistic nature of her life. And if you
can fulfill all three of those desires, you have a much
higher likelihood of retaining her.[53]*

In other words, help the woman in the middle take professional development very personally, and watch the virtuous cycle spin.

And last, but definitely not least, leveraging your existing employee resource groups is a smart, low-cost way to bring very personal professional development opportunities to all of your employees.

Allbirds, maker of "the world's most comfortable shoe," helps employees grow and develop as people by bringing important and relevant content to their ERGs.

One such group, called Mom&Pop Birds is for parents and caregivers. It includes those employees who work in the retail stores, which Allbirds understands is a particularly stretched subset of employees. Laura Mallers, senior director of external reporting and internal controls and cochair of the Mom&Pop Birds ERG, shared with me that the focus is to "support parents via opportunities to hold discussions and ask questions, bring in speakers on relevant topics, and inform relevant policy decisions."[54]

I had the pleasure to attend a recent Mom&Pop Birds event, where Allbirds brought in Audrey Wisch, the cofounder and CEO of Curious Cardinals, an EdTech company that helps connect middle and high school students with mentors. Wisch spoke to parents about how to help kids find their passion (talk about starting professional development early!); Mallers chose this topic as a way of offering "tactical advice and ideas, but also something that celebrates the joy of parenting."[55] Because I was there, I could see the magic for myself—not only were employees learning valuable information about their kids and getting parenting tips, they saw that they were not alone in their challenges, and they were getting to know each other in new ways.

Think about the opportunities in your organization to grow—through a stipend, taking a class, participating in a lunch and learn, or hearing a speaker in one of the employee resource groups that you don't typically attend. Next time you have an opportunity to participate, think about how you can grow beyond your day job and develop more broadly as a person.

That's the power of growing from the inside out—together.

PS: Happier at Zapier

Like many (OK . . . most) tech companies, hiring in 2023 has slowed at Zapier. But instead of laying off employees like so many of their competitors, Chief People Officer Brandon Sammut has other plans. As he told the *Modern People Leader* podcast, "Our number one focus for 2023, talent-wise, is what we call talent density."

What does that mean? It means they "help the people we just hired realize their potential."[56]

One of the many reasons people are "happier at Zapier" (beyond just a reminder of how to pronounce the company name) is because they are taking the long view of talent redeployment, even during times of layoffs. Sammut created a "secondment program," defined as "the temporary assignment of an employee from one organization to another for a specified period of time, usually to carry out a particular project. It can be an intracompany transfer within the same organization or between two unrelated business entities."[57]

As Zapier's recruiting manager, Bonnie Dilber, put it, "At Zapier, we care deeply about everyone and know their potential and ability go far beyond their core job they are hired to do."[58] With secondments, they're able to reallocate talent to parts of the business with a high need.[59]

Based on three factors—business needs, skills match, and employee interest—Zapier placed team members from talent acquisition into projects in other areas of the business. Dilber explains, "While our team was focused first and foremost on meeting the needs of the business, we didn't want anyone to feel pressured to work on projects that didn't align with their interests and goals. And I'm proud to say that we accomplished that, with each team member landing in one of their top-choice projects."[60]

Dilber also recognizes that for some of their team members, this temporary reassignment may lead to a new career path. She thinks that's great: "Their experience in talent acquisition will make them that much more valuable no matter what they do, and we're thrilled to be able to play a role in accelerating their path into other fields."[61]

And, if someone is not "happier at Zapier," they've created a program called the "Next Play Program," which you'll read about in Chapter Seven.

Besides their Next Play Program, Zapier has several other ways to engage with employees and help them continue to grow in their career paths. Sammut told me, "This includes sharing new jobs first in the internal job board before broadly opening it up to external candidates. It also includes having employees create formalized but optional career growth plans, which encourages folks to identify key career moments they'd like to achieve and provide steps on how to achieve them while here at Zapier."[62] They also utilize Zapier's "Career Pathways" program, which helps employees learn about and pursue roles at Zapier outside their current team and growth trajectory.

"Here at Zapier, we understand that careers aren't always linear and that sometimes people find something else that excites them," Sammut shared with me. "Where possible, we want to give people options to explore their career passions here at Zapier."[63]

That's a (W)RAP

Retention Action Plan for Professional Development

1. Make a list of development opportunities you currently offer your employees. People want to grow on the job—up, down, or sideways. If you're having trouble getting buy-in from the top, remember professional development is a competitive business advantage, so share the data.

2. Encourage managers to have regular conversations with their employees about how they want to grow and develop. Be specific! Communicate that hoarding talent is not good for people or business. Having these conversations and supporting growth plans is critical to retain top talent.

3. Look inside your organization for development opportunities. Maybe it's through a stipend for classes, access to online learning (e.g., LinkedIn, Coursera, or Udemy), a lunch and learn with a guest speaker, employee resource group (ERG) programming, or an internal-ship. Maybe you offer dedicated time in another part of the business to expand employees' knowledge. It's important to keep in mind that development opportunities should take place *during the workday*!

4. Bake professional development into the very beginning of the employee journey. Why wait to start growing your employees? Find out as early as onboarding how an employee envisions growing with and for the organization, and make a plan with them, tailored to their goals.

5. No strings attached! Yep, even though you're offering opportunities right off the bat. Start early, and don't worry about developing people right out the door, either. In the virtuous cycle of the Retention Revolution, you never know when they'll come back around to you with new clients, new business, or even a request to return as a boomerang employee.

CHAPTER SIX

MANAGERS ARE HAVING A MOMENT

Why You Should Invest in Your Most Valuable Employees

> ### OLD IDEA #6
>
> Managers are in the messy middle of their career and your organization—and are easily overlooked.
>
> ### NEW BEGINNING #6
>
> Managers should be elevated and celebrated.

You've probably heard the oft-quoted 2015 Gallup gospel, "people don't leave companies, they leave managers."[1] But today, this is not just an important idea to keep in mind, it's a make-or-break truth. A 2022 GoodHire survey of 3,000 Americans found that "82% of American workers said they would potentially quit their job because of a bad manager."[2]

Managers are always important, but in the Retention Revolution, they're your MVP.

Unfortunately, as recent headlines highlight the difficulty of this important role ("The Plight of the Middle Manager,"[3] "The Middle Managers Are Not Alright,"[4] "Why Middle Managers Are Feeling the Squeeze and How to Fix It,"[5] "How Flexibility Made Managers Miserable,"[6] "No One Wants to Be a Middle Manager Anymore"[7]), it makes sense that talented people might want to skip right over this step on the corporate ladder.

As Denise Rousseau, professor of organizational behavior and public policy at Carnegie Mellon University, points out, "The name gives it away: middle managers are caught in the middle, they have to deal with issues up and down an organization."[8] When they're feeling pressure from all sides—and who isn't these days?!—it's no wonder so many managers are feeling burned out and stressed out.

Research from Slack's Future Forum confirms that a whopping 43 percent of middle managers are "at high risk for burnout."[9] And in Gallup chairman Jim Clifton's book *It's the Manager*, he notes that "Managers report more stress and burnout, worse work-life balance, and worse physical wellbeing than the individual contributors on the teams they lead."[10]

These days managers are being relied upon even more by their direct reports, which is yet another reason why their well-being is so central to the health and well-being of your organization. Nowadays, nearly 70 percent of people say their manager had "the greatest impact on their mental health, on par with the impact of their partner."[11]

In fact, a Salesforce survey found "employees rate their immediate supervisor as most important to understanding the organization and its priorities, above the executive team."[12] And as Cara Allamano, chief people officer at Lattice, explains, "[The manager's] job has become even more important in the last two to three years because they truly are that connection between the broader business, the broader organization, the broader culture, and individuals who want to do a good job in their work."[13]

The impact of the manager is broad, yes, but it is also a laser-focused solution for the problem of retention. In one Gallup study, "Fifty-two percent of voluntarily exiting employees say their manager or organization could have done something to prevent them from leaving their job."[14] That's a huge percentage of people who could've been retained had there been regular, ongoing conversations about their employee experience.

Which is to say that training your managers has an exponential effect. As individual contributors, managers have an outsized impact on the state of your workforce, so you'd be wise to focus on their training and feedback in order to keep your company healthy.

Also, to state the (perhaps) obvious, managers are employees, too. In other words, in the Retention Revolution, managers are really having a moment, and you should do everything you can to help them lead others and themselves well.

Your company's success depends on it.

Elevate and Celebrate

In my many years of research on the human workplace, especially during turbulent times, I've come to appreciate the importance of shifts in perception. Of course, we need programs, procedures, and protocols. The rubber definitely needs to meet the road. But until we know what we value and *why* we value it, our actions won't have the impact we hope they will.

This has never been more true than it is with the role of the manager.

As the very definition of work and the employee journey shifts, this is the time to reevaluate and reestablish the role of the manager in your organization.

What does this mean?

It means that instead of just plugging people into this incredibly important position because they're so good at their day job (e.g., the salesperson who is so good at selling that she gets promoted to sales manager), or because there's a vacancy and they're available, everyone will benefit when you take the role of the manager seriously.

You do this by elevating and then celebrating.

First of all, you want your managers' programs to be a *thing*. I'm sure you're already offering *something* for your new (and existing) managers, but my guess is that it's not enough. I encourage you to take a good look at the process of becoming a manager in your organization and elevate it. Give it a name and a real, professional process. Create a cool, branded experience that aligns with the mission of the company, and then shout it from the rooftops. Don't be shy.

The next thing you'll want to do is celebrate the role. One of the main ways to do this is by creating community (It's hard to celebrate alone, right?) Again, I'm guessing you already have a Slack channel or similar way to bring new managers together, but I think you'll be very happy to see what happens when you elevate that, too, into a full-blown community experience. There's nothing better than learning with a truly connected cohort that moves together through the elevated experience of becoming amazing managers.

The Year of the Manager at Kraft Heinz

When Melissa Werneck, global chief people officer at Kraft Heinz Company, heard the Gallup stat that only 1 in 10 people is naturally wired to be a manager,[15] she decided, "We need to dedicate more time to listening, feedback, [and] training."[16]

In other words, she knew it was time to elevate managers. Big time.

After an internal survey revealed that "80% of employees wanted their leaders to be better coaches, and 92% of leaders wanted to be better coaches for their employees,"[17] Werneck decided to call 2022 "the year of the manager."[18]

She understands just how much responsibility managers have, especially in this hybrid world—"we ask a lot of our managers."[19] So, Kraft built an all-encompassing manager development strategy, starting by launching Project WIN, a perfect example of a loud-and-proud program for managers.

Project WIN (which stands for "Work as a Team, Inspire Excellence, and Navigate Our Future") is a worldwide initiative to develop great managers at all levels of the organization. Inspired by Google's Project Oxygen, an internal research project to determine what qualities make a great manager, their main objective is to transform managers into amazing coaches by leading with empathy and care, moving with speed and agility, and growing people to their full potential.

And Werneck tells HR Brew, a popular newsletter among HR professionals, "[Managers] are not only engaged and think they are becoming better managers, [but] employees are saying that they are becoming better managers."[20]

What are the results? Werneck says they've seen better employee engagement, performance, and—no big surprise—retention.[21]

| THE **SWEET SPOT** |
| BETWEEN **TECH & CONNECT** |

HUMU

Even the best managers may need a nudge.
     When leaders receive training on how to be more human, they still need support. They're only human after all! Sometimes we all need a little nudge. According to the authors Richard H. Thaler and Cass R. Sunstein, a nudge is "any aspect of the choice architecture that alters people's behavior in a predictable way without forbidding any options or significantly changing their economic incentives." So, critically, "nudges are not mandates."[22]

The concept of the nudge is the impetus behind Humu, a software platform (and the company detailed in Chapter One) that uses technology to help leaders guide high-performing teams. Humu's mission: To create a workplace where every manager is great. Who wouldn't want that!?

I wanted to know more about what makes the nudge, so I spoke with one of my favorite authors and former head of communications and content at Humu, Liz Fosslien.

Fosslien shared that the fundamental idea for the nudge at Humu is, "getting people in moments that matter, when it's easiest to take action, and making it really, really simple for them to make the next best decision." Because Humu knows that "seemingly small changes in behavior have a large impact on how people feel they can show up at work."[23] And showing up as our most appropriate, authentic human self—as this book has hopefully made clear—*really* matters!

One of the primary use cases for the nudge is around supporting leaders. Companies will come to Humu and say, "Managers are really stretched thin, how can we help them to remember to invest in the soft skills?" Imagine you want to be able to share vulnerably with your manager. How much easier would it be to feel like you're in a safe, supportive one-on-one environment with them if you know they're being supported, too? One example of a nudge for an upcoming one-on-one for a manager could be: "In this one-on-one, try opening with, What one thing can I do to better support you this week?" At the same time, a nudge is sent to the direct report asking them to "think of a way that your manager can support you this week." Using nudges to help managers and employees alike build their soft skills helps everyone feel safer and more human.

The Stuff That Matters at O.C. Tanner

O.C. Tanner, the employee recognition company we met in Chapter Five, is very intentional about how they train their managers. They know full well that, as Chief Marketing and People Officer Mindi Cox says, "an employee's experience with [managers] *is* their O.C. Tanner experience."[24] The leaders at O.C. Tanner very much understand this, and they build their entire culture around supporting managers. "Everything we do ought to be in support of those leaders, those middle managers, those frontline leaders. We can only scale the impact of culture through them."

And O.C. Tanner also recognizes that most of a manager's time and attention should be given to the people side of their role. When Cox asked a newly promoted manager how things were going, the manager replied, "I'm so grateful for this opportunity, but I can't get anything done! These people are in my face all day long, asking me to solve this problem or that problem, and I just can't get to the work anymore." Cox responded, "All of *that* stuff is the work now."[25] As in, the people are your work now. As they should be! Because "expectations change when you're elevated into a leader role."[26]

A regular employee's *stuff* is the manager's bread and butter.

The Journey at General Mills

All the way back in 2018, General Mills began what they call their "Engaging Leader" (EL) program. The people team spoke with managers and asked, "What would it take for you to be a great leader? What do you need?"

In response, according to General Mills CHRO Jacqueline Williams-Roll, the managers asked for "language, learning, and tools to help them bring our General Mills values to life in their day-to-day interactions with their teams and be the best manager they could be."[27]

Who wouldn't want to give managers like that exactly what they asked for?

Because managers requested a way to check their own progress, Williams-Roll put in place an Engaging Leader survey that allows direct reports to "share how they're doing and how they're growing" through a variety of ways, including question cards, community forums, and manager cohorts. Yep, all the smart things. They then proceeded to train 4,400 leaders around the world based on what employees shared. As I often say, to lead a human workplace, you must get your values "off the walls" and "into the halls." And General Mills gets it. As Williams-Roll explained, "Everything is very much aligned to our values. In essence what Engaging Leader is, is 'How do we bring our values to life?' "[28]

Herein lies the heart of their very elevated *and celebrated* manager journey.

The program begins by taking managers through the company's core values (win together, continuously innovate, champion belonging, do the right thing all the time) and then gives them actionable reflection and practice on what that looks like.

In one example of living the value of winning together, managers clearly lay out their strategic intent and what efforts support it. They are explicit about the who and the what, and the rules and responsibilities. Managers are asked to reflect on how well they're doing in each area, and they're also given feedback from their direct reports. The CEO is fully onboard with the work, too. Every year he picks three EL behaviors he wants the organization to improve on for the year, based on their business strategy and engagement survey.

This is a full-scale elevation.

Finally, as a means of celebration, every year General Mills holds the Engaging Leader "Champions Awards" where they recognize three to five people who are role models for Engaging Leader behaviors. These champions are then put into a cohort for the following year, where they act as an internal focus group (more community!). Leadership will test new concepts with the cohort, leverage them to teach other managers, and bring them in front of the global officers once a year to have the cohort speak on what they're doing to be engaging leaders themselves and what they need from *their* leaders.

And it really does make a difference. Williams-Roll shared, "Eighty-eight percent of our people feel like they're supported by their manager. And that has a direct correlation with not only engagement, but retention and how people are talking about our brand externally."[29]

General Mills's manager program is a true investment in the ecosystem of opportunity.

Banfield Pet Hospital Helps People, Too

Veterinarians enter the profession because of their passion for helping pets and the people who love them, but for some, the *people* part of the job doesn't come as naturally to them. New graduates start their careers ready to dive into practicing medicine, but sometimes they are not as prepared for the dynamics that come with being part of a team, taking on leadership roles, or managing tough client interactions. Yet, despite dedicating their lives to the health and well-being of pets, veterinarians also need to feel connected to their colleagues, their organizations, and their profession.

And, they need to learn how to be managers.

Mars Chief Medical Officer Dr. Molly McAllister shared with me that a few years back Banfield heard that their doctors felt a disconnect between staff and leaders within the company. They were looking for local leadership, with whom to communicate and check in. Like anyone else, they wanted to have someone there to understand their unique needs and what they were going through. As McAllister told me, "One of the main pieces of feedback we were hearing from our doctors was that they wanted stronger connections with local leadership."[30]

Which is another way of saying, of course, that managers needed to be elevated.

To address this issue, in January 2020, Banfield formalized a new chief of staff role in their hospitals. This person is a trained veterinarian who spends 50 percent of their time seeing patients and 50 percent of their time managing hospital teams in their assigned region. Because the area chiefs of staff are doctors, they can empathize and lead hospital teams through stressors and challenges, and they can take a pulse on how the hospital is feeling.

Wisely, instead of just creating a new position and hoping for the best, Banfield really elevates this new role and celebrates it by creating community around it. They provide extensive training on how to lead with empathy, as well as how to create in-person and virtual opportunities to share best practices. And they're even teaching some area chiefs of staff to be facilitators and to train others.

McAllister shared that, though these leaders are not always common in the veterinary field, the ones who find themselves in the role have come to her overwhelmed with emotion because they say the role is so perfect for them. "They'll say things like, 'This is the job I've wanted my whole career.'"[31]

So, what do they do to create community? A lot!

They hold town halls and quarterly training on topics like health and wellness, financial literacy, and relevant topics such as creating psychological safety. Banfield also offers regional gatherings, either in person or remote. And finally, two cohort communities are the icing on the community cake. One is larger and comes together for in-depth, peer-to-peer development in small breakout groups. This larger cohort also discusses topics that really focus on leadership skills such as prioritization, managing difficult conversations, action planning, and more. The second cohort is a smaller group of chiefs of staff who have gone through the program previously. These folks facilitate and help lead conversations in some of the sessions. It's an opportunity for them to further their own skills and help others grow. A win-win!

After implementing this new role in the hospitals, elevating it, and celebrating it, the results have been amazing, though not surprising. Turnover is down, and Banfield has been able to create more sustainability in a notoriously understaffed field. The doctors who feel connected to their manager . . . they stick around.

Model, Coach, Care with Microsoft

At the World Economic Forum at Davos in 2022, Satya Nadella talked about the role of the manager in a very powerful way. Referring to the way Covid forced all of us into a "crisis together," he said, "just before we went into the pandemic, Microsoft had this management training program we put in place called Model, Coach, Care. I must say it was just great timing because caring became the currency during the pandemic . . . every manager had to care for the connection they had with their people."[32]

The truth is that managers always have to care, but when someone like Nadella elevates and celebrates this aspect of their job, it makes it much more possible.

He continued, "So if you asked me this, what is that leadership quality that I think each of us has to build more muscle in? It's that caring."[33]

So how does Model, Coach, Care work?

Joe Whittinghill, Microsoft's corporate vice president of talent, learning and insights, wanted to consolidate their management model. So, they conducted two years of research and testing and came up with a neuroscience-based program, which they called Model, Coach, Care. Microsoft rolled out the program in 2019. Sure, Microsoft is one of the biggest companies in the world, but that doesn't mean you can't emulate their process by doing some research on your own and then creating a program that works for you.

Model, Coach, Care is a two-pronged approach: empowering managers and holding them accountable. Whittinghill told me how they approached redefining the manager's role at Microsoft: "These three—model, coach, and care—are the most critical to managers' success, whether it be with each individual team member or leading productive, connected, and inclusive teams. Beyond this model being clear, concise, and easy to remember for our managers the dual power has been that employees are clear on what they can expect of their managers."[34]

I love the idea of managers using Model, Coach, Care with their teams, but I wanted to know how Microsoft cares for its managers, so I asked Whittinghill to explain. He told me about yet another layer of care they're taking with the entire manager community, which of course begins with creating community.

Community forums happen several times a year and are—interestingly—run by managers themselves, not HR.

How do the managers feel about being elevated and celebrated?

"We've gotten some great feedback that these forums act like a 'pressure release valve' and bring comfort and camaraderie in that they are not alone in their challenges and successes here at Microsoft."[35]

When managers let off steam together, everyone in the company can relax.

Here's the good news: if you are intrigued by this Model, Coach, Care program, you can take the course yourself. As it was rolled out to the more than 18,000 managers, Microsoft leadership got so much positive feedback and questions about the program that they decided to open-source the content. Now anyone and everyone can learn how to manage like the managers at Microsoft, through a free course on LinkedIn Learning.

Upwork's Call for Community

Upwork, the online work marketplace, has approximately 2,700 full-time and hybrid team members combined. Upwork CEO Hayden Brown thinks a lot about managers and asks smart questions, such as, "What does performance management look like? What does the role of the manager look like? How do we reward and retain people in a world where these rules have changed so fundamentally?"[36]

When I asked her what she thinks the new role of the manager looks like, she made it clear that she was serious about elevating the manager by "re-engaging and activating the managers in the business."[37] And how does she plan on doing that?

By creating community, of course.

Once a month, managers join forces with Brown for a meeting on Zoom called the "One Upwork Forum." As Brown told me, "We have this rallying cry of the business that we [try to] only solve problems in the best and most brilliant way through working together as One Upwork."[38]

During this elevated call for community, managers share information with Brown via a Q&A, but there's also a peer-to-peer element. They have "very candid discussions where people are talking about change management that they're driving, or how things are going and certain DEI initiatives, what they're struggling with, [and] tactics and tips across each other."[39] The conversation also continues in a Slack channel, where managers can post and stay updated on all things Upwork.

While this is a peer-to-peer call, it's sponsored by a rotating executive every six months, someone who, as Brown told me, is "willing to nurture and be the voice and the champion" of the group. They've seen this as a "really great way to drive that engagement and have that group helping each other, as they've gone through so much change."[40]

Together.

Managers Squared

Squarespace has seen incredible growth during the pandemic.[41] And like so many in their enviable position, it's quite a challenge to keep everyone up to speed, especially when the people being promoted to management have expertise in their field but not a lot of training in management, per se.

Andrew Stern, who looks after Squarespace's manager development and coaching investments, shared how their comprehensive programs—for the managers of managers, or managers squared—elevate the heck out of the role:

Let's say I am a new manager at Squarespace. Sure, of course you would expect Squarespace to give you skills, give you a network, give you a community, no doubt. But we take it one step further to say the manager of that new manager needs to be upskilled in how they can be most supportive to that new manager, and what the new manager is learning.[42]

See how Stern refers to a community for managers as table stakes? He's absolutely right!

And Stern knows that it's not enough to just send managers—or their manager's managers—through a cookie-cutter program. It needs to be just as well-considered as any other product in the company. When you remember, like Stern does, to treat employees like valued customers, it becomes clear that a one-size-fits-all training will fall short.

As Stern explained, "It's this notion of personalization, customization, relevance, specificity. We experience it in so many elements of our day-to-day life . . . it's been staring us in the face for the past two and a half years during the pandemic, whether it's Netflix, or Spotify, or Amazon. It's these curated, personalized experiences on these platforms. And the same must be true for learning and development investments as we go forward."[43]

Imagine a world where we log in to our work portal and get notifications based on our preferences and the professional development content we've finished, loved, and even shared: "Hi Erica, we think you're going to love this course on the manager!"

That future is closer than you might think.

Learning how to elevate and celebrate your managers can take time because it comes from a shift in perspective. So at the end of the day, what really matters is relationships—between managers and their teams, managers and leaders, and managers and themselves.

As Dr. Ella Washington, Georgetown professor and author of *The Necessary Journey*, shared at the October 2022 Future Forum conference, "Connecting with employees is often seen as 'extra' work for managers, so it goes to the bottom of the list. Companies need to make it clear—it is not extra; it is essential."[44]

At the heart of the human workplace is the idea of honoring relationships, so people are always at the center of every successful company. But the Retention Revolution insists that we connect with individuals on an intentional, regular basis. The best way to begin this important work is to take note of all the ways people *already* interact at work and turn up the volume—strategically, professionally, and personally.

That's a (W)RAP

Retention Action Plan for Managers

1. Managers are having a moment. As we know, people don't leave jobs, they leave managers. That's why we need to treat managers as the MVPs of our organizations.

2. Elevate your manager program. Build a robust and formalized training program to ensure your managers are adequately supported in this kind of role, especially if they're coming into management from an individual contributor role.

3. Align the development of managers and the management model back to company values. If everyone is leveling up through the same framework—a.k.a. your values—your organization will see better cohesion, horizontally and vertically. And, it's another way to bring your values to life.

4. Celebrate managers through community, connection, and recognition. Middle managers often feel especially overwhelmed and underappreciated. Make sure you celebrate their wins and cultivate opportunities for connection with other managers so they can feel supported by their peers.

5. Lead the way. Model the behavior you want to see your managers exhibit with their direct reports. Provide the same connection, empowerment, coaching, and empathy you want them to show their team members.

CHAPTER SEVEN

OFFBOARDING AS YOU MEAN TO GO ON (AND ON)

OLD IDEA #7

There's the door. Don't let it hit you. . . .

NEW BEGINNING #7

Smart companies know how to get a positive return on employee churn.

t's 3 p.m. in Seattle, Washington, the perfect time for a pick-me-up.

A small group sits around a table at Starbucks' headquarters, with a woman at the front of the room describing the differences between the two cups of coffee in front of her. She tells the people about the subtleties of the brews. She shares the beans' origin stories and makes suggestions about what she'd like to see them paired with—a blueberry scone perhaps? The small crowd is riveted, faces leaning over their own steaming cups of coffee, sipping their drinks, relishing it. One man looks especially connected to his cup. You can see that he's really savoring it, taking it all in.

This scene is from what's called the "First Sip," part of an onboarding ritual that happens at Starbucks locations all around the world. And it's something people remember well, even years later, in great detail:

> *I remember having a delicious cup of LightNote Blend . . . [in] 1998.*
>
> *I remember . . . having my mind blown.*
>
> *One year ago on the 25th of September . . . I believe I tried either Sumatra or Cafe Verona.*

But this time is different.

Instead of the usual onboarding experience, this First Sip is a bittersweet celebration of an executive leaving the company after many years. The aforementioned gentleman communing with his coffee isn't saying goodbye in retirement, either. He's leaving for a different job.

And he's being celebrated.

Beyond onboarding or offboarding, this First Sip is a new beginning.

Starbucks, by any measure, is one of the most successful companies in the world today. It also happens to be a big part of the one thing I do every day—"One tall, extra hot soy latte, please!"

I began my first book with a story about Ashley Peterson, the Starbucks barista who showed me what it meant to bring her human to work. I ended my second book, *Rituals Roadmap*, with a deep dive into Starbucks rituals. It's only fitting that my third book—the final in my Human Workplace trilogy—should also feature Starbucks.

I'm truly impressed and inspired by the way every one of their 350,000 partners—baristas, accountants, administrators—begin their employee journey with the First Sip. At Starbucks, this ritual is how every new partner starts their career, highlighting the passion that everyone at the company has for coffee and the magic it brings to themselves and their customers.

But that's just the beginning.

Imagine being honored with your company's most sacred ritual as you walk out the door! Contrast that feeling to the "Joey Quits" viral video of a guy who was so eager to leave his job at a hotel that he brought in a marching band to play as he told his boss, "I quit!"[1]

Consider how celebrated that first employee will feel about their ex-employer versus Joey as they move into the world—as talent, as a consumer, as a potential client, as a human being. Which company would you rather be as your ex-employee moves into their next position, then the next, then the next?

Imagine unlocking the golden handcuffs and wishing your top talent well as they mosey into different—if not greener—pastures.

Imagine even planning for their exit as they enter.

Imagine actually helping your superstars find new jobs.

Imagine offering no strings attached sabbaticals and professional development that's truly personal, an offering that may develop them right out the door.

Imagine creating tech that supports employees as customers, seeking assignments that align with their ever-shifting goals.

And then, imagine how gratified you'll feel if your top talent recommends their friends and even asks for their old job back.

In 2008, Howard Schultz rejoined Starbucks as CEO for his second tour of duty, bringing the company back from the brink with a 143 percent stock jump.[2]

In 2022, Disney, looking for a solution to their streaming problem and an industry crippled by the pandemic, brought back Bob Iger.

And who could forget when Steve Jobs returned to Apple in 1997 after being pushed out in 1985?

Not every boomerang CEO works magic, but there is certainly a business case to be made for leaving the door open when successful employees—at all levels—leave your company.

In fact, these days, LinkedIn is filled with posts from companies including Deutsche Bank AG, EY, and Deloitte touting returning employees, often with elaborate blog posts, pictures, and videos showing happy staff back at their companies. Quite a contrast to the before times, when off-boarding was pretty much just onboarding in reverse: Give the keys and the company-issued laptop back, maybe sign up for some vague alumni networking opportunities, set up a "You can reach me at . . . " email and, if you are one of the lucky ones, your colleagues might toast to your goodbye at a company happy hour. Oh . . . and don't let the door hit you on the way out.

Smart companies today are thrilled when ex-employees want to make a comeback. According to Bloomberg News, the CEO of engineering and tech recruitment firm Gattaca plc, Matthew Wragg, has hired "six boomerang employees in the past three months." As Wragg put it, "They know the culture. They know the operating processes."[3]

According to a study[4] conducted by John Arnold, assistant professor at the University of Missouri, boomerang employees are pretty reliable. Arnold and a group of researchers examined some 30,000 boomerang and traditional employees over eight years and found that in general, there wasn't a lot of change in performance between stints.

Research from *Harvard Business Review* gives us more insight on who these recent boomerangs are and why they returned. They found that, "Across organizations in a wide range of industries, 28% of 'new hires' were actually boomerang hires who had resigned within the last 36 months."[5] What's more, most boomerangs tend to go back to their previous employer within 13 months.

So, why did these employees decide to return? "Employees felt that their new organization did not live up to the promises it made or the expectations it set when they were hired."[6] In other words, the grass isn't always greener. Sometimes, it's brown! And let's not forget, "the more workers maintained strong social ties to their former colleagues, the more likely they were to return."[7] All this means that if you offboard well and stay connected to your former employees, there may be a chance in the future to welcome them back with open arms.

Amy Spurling, founder and CEO of employment perk startup Compt, told me, "Sometimes an employee has to leave a company to continue their career growth. The best leaders recognize and support this because it's not a sign of disloyalty, rather it's someone who is motivated to develop professionally. If that person decides to come back to your organization in the future, any experiences they had elsewhere could make them that much more valuable to the team."[8]

I would go so far as to say that boomerang employees are actually one of the best-kept secrets of the Retention Revolution—evidence that opening the doors and letting go of expectations is good for business.

To attract boomerangs, it's important to first reevaluate how you think about employee departures, to make sure that when beloved employees leave—because they will!—their exit doesn't fall flat.

According to Laura Coccaro, chief people officer at iCIMS, "Offboarding an employee is just as important as onboarding in the age of the boomerang."[9]

Or, as some folks refer to it, give employees a "red carpet in and a red carpet out."

As important as boomerangs are, they aren't the only reason you want to create royal exit strategies. Remember, in the

Retention Revolution, we're harnessing the power of human potential *beyond* the traditional terms of employment. As Steve Cadigan writes in *Workquake*, "Organizations need to shift their thinking from 'How do we keep our staff from leaving?' and move it toward 'How do we make our people better for an uncertain future?' "[10]

Nobody's future is certain, and ultimately and truly, we're all in this together.

Indeed, once an employee moves on, their intelligence and energy are still on the table as a boomerang, as we've seen, but also as brand ambassador, referral source, and even a client. While we can't know exactly what the relationship will ultimately look like, by understanding offboarding as the new onboarding (to a new phase of your relationship), you'll create the conditions for, perhaps, a safe and inspired return, a lifetime of goodwill, or at the very least, a feeling of connection.

As Daniel Kahneman, psychologist and recipient of the 2002 Nobel Memorial Prize in Economic Sciences, explains in his peak-end rule theory, people generally judge an experience based on how they felt at its peak and how they felt at the end of the experience. These feelings tend to cloud everything else out. This reminds me, yet again, of when my kids were little and we hosted play dates and birthday parties. As hard as it was to say goodbye, I always tried to shut it down when all the kids were having a blast instead of waiting until they were ready to go (i.e., having a meltdown).

As an employer, you also want to avoid meltdowns at all costs (too bad nobody told the "Crying CEO" from Chapter Three) and for your soon-to-be-ex-employee/brand ambassador to leave with a good taste in their mouth. After all, the way your employees feel at the end sends a message not just to the person leaving, but to all of those who are staying.

According to Gallup, employees who have a positive exit experience are 2.9 times *more* likely to recommend that organization to others.[11] Unfortunately, far too often, people wait until the actual exit to gather the information that might have forestalled the exit in the first place.

As bestselling author and Wharton Professor Adam Grant says, "I'm a big fan of exit interviews. Just one little issue: it is the dumbest time to run them." In a popular LinkedIn post from January 2023, he sang the praises of the entry interview for new employees as well as the stay interview for current employees, as ways to ask, " 'Why are you here?' 'What are you hoping to learn?' 'What are some of the best projects you've worked on?' 'Tell me about the worst boss you've ever had.' . . . 'What has been the defining highlight of your experience here?' 'What have been the low lights?' 'What made you consider quitting and how do we make sure that doesn't happen again?' "[12]

I love these ideas. And as the smart users of LinkedIn pointed out en masse, if we want any of these questions to work, we need to create a culture where people will want to open up—anytime.

As one reader of Grant's post commented:

While I agree that these questions should be asked throughout an employee's employment, I think much of this comes down to the culture of an organization and whether it actually cares about retention as much as it might say it does and whether it's willing to put in the hard work to make employees stay. (Niti Nadarajah)

And another:

Great contribution Adam Grant 👏 The exit interviews at the end of the employment relationship is indeed the worst timing. And it all boils down to the outdated corporate mentality where people are expendable 😔, they are just numbers on a sheet that could be replaced with new numbers. (Yaroslava Vovk)

Again and again, people like the readers above pointed to how important it is for companies to foster a sense of psychological safety throughout the employee's journey in order to get real answers from anyone who wants to stay in the company's orbit. This is, of course, what we want from a Retention Revolution point of view.

The so-called end of the employee journey is one of the most important moments in this revolution, upon which this virtuous cycle turns. And while maybe it goes without saying, of course you'll reserve the royal treatment for employees leaving on good terms.

So how exactly do we breathe new life into endings and offboarding, so that employees want to stay connected? You start by being intentional—by offboarding as you mean to go on. And just like we did with onboarding, you do that by making it Professional, Purposeful, and Personal.

Take Offboarding Professionally

Taking offboarding professionally means assigning someone to own the process—soup to nuts—the same way you would a new product line or marketing strategy. The same way you do with onboarding.

Why? Because offboarding is big business and deserves to be treated with a professional touch.

According to Jenifer Andrasko, executive vice president and global head of alumni at Bain & Company Inc. (and a boomerang employee herself), during offboarding their departure partner helps exiting "Bainies" connect to "alumni in their fields of interest and job opportunities at sought-after organizations, in addition to giving them access to external career coaches."[13] Pretty incredible, huh? Giving someone coaching after they've left your company?

Why would you want to do that?

Because, Andrasko continues, "Ensuring that departing employees leave well, meaning that they feel supported at departure, results in them being five times more likely to be promoters of the firm."[14]

That's why.

Colleagues for Life at Kirkland & Ellis

What if you took professionalizing offboarding to a whole new level? At law firm Kirkland & Ellis LLP, they've built robust programs, including their Alumni Engagement Program, Kirkland CareerLink (KCL), and Kirkland Concierge to support their alumni, because "Whether an attorney retires from the Firm or leaves as an associate, Kirkland appreciates their contribution and will continue to invest in their career." They also know that, as Chiara Wrocinski, chief administrative officer (and former alumni engagement director), told me, "As buyers, consumers, and influencers, their [alumni's] reach is powerful."[15]

Within these programs, the attorneys and alumni have access to a networking directory and website, free continuing legal education support, lifelong career support, and exclusive discounts on services. Specifically, in the CareerLink program, they offer former and current attorneys confidential coaching, career-focused events, secondments, clerkships, and transfers to in-house positions.[16]

CareerLink builds long-term relationships with their people through "in-depth career coaching, innovative program and resource development, and network building."[17] And this is regardless of tenure length or status because they're dedicated to remaining colleagues for life.

And finally, although this is certainly nice to have, it's not a must-have, the firm offers Kirkland Concierge, which helps their people, both current and former, take care of their personal to-do lists, like "travel planning, gift buying, product comparison research, moving assistance, pet care referrals, and more." And on-site amenities include dry cleaning, shoe shining, gift wrapping around the holidays, car washes, and yes, even haircuts. Wow. We know that lawyers are very busy people, so this kind of service makes total sense to help them alleviate some of those annoying, time-draining tasks. But I'm still blown away that this is offered to alumni as well.

So why go to all this trouble? As Wrocinski put it, "The firm knows many of our attorneys will move on, taking their skills and relationships into the marketplace—for so many reasons we want to keep our connections close."[18] Alumni who have found positions on in-house legal teams via Career-Link have brought referrals and clients back to the firm.[19] So, clearly there's your business case for professionalizing your offboarding.

NO MATTER HOW
HIGH- OR LOW-TECH

Many human companies likely use HR software throughout an employee's journey—from recruiting and onboarding, to professional development and learning opportunities, to compliance and paperwork, all the way to offboarding and moving on. And these comprehensive tools are amazing! But I actually think that the most important time to use any tool is in offboarding. Why? Because in the Retention Revolution, this is your time to shine!

Of course, we want to be intentional in connection all throughout the employee journey, but if you don't do it during offboarding, you may not get another chance. Sometimes that connection is as simple as a low-tech email newsletter or database of former employees. Take LinkedIn's alumni newsletter, for example, which I'll describe later. It's such a simple tool, yet it keeps all former employees in the loop. Or Microsoft's *Beyond the Blue Badge* podcast for alumni—it's an easy, low-tech way to stay connected to what former employees are up to. My previous firm, Booz Allen Hamilton, taps former employees through a database "to fill short-term, temporary, and project-based staffing needs."[20]

Of course, you can also scale all the way up to a more high-tech solution, like an online alumni portal. Accenture has a platform where its more than 400,000 alumni can access rehire and referral programs, participate in

> exclusive webinars and events, and stay connected to current and former colleagues.[21] So, no matter how high- or low-tech your alumni offerings are, staying connected to your former employees is a very powerful way to keep the revolving door of opportunity in motion.

Offboard on Purpose

In *Bring Your Human to Work*, long before the pandemic and the Retention Revolution, I interviewed Harry Nathan Gottlieb, the founder of Jellyvision, the Chicago-based benefits software company, about their ahead-of-its-time "graceful leaving" policy.

Here's how it works: as soon as employees begin their journey at Jellyvision, they're asked to consider their end.

Why?

For the sake of those left to fill in the holes at the end of an employee's tenure, but also for the employees themselves, who won't have to skulk around in the shadows, afraid to share their big news. In exchange for their transparency, employees get the support of Jellyvision in their job search, contacts and introductions, and even résumé assistance.

And we know what Jellyvision gets: a whole lot of happy ex-employees out there, spreading good cheer about their company.

More than just a way to create smooth transitions, graceful leave is the quintessential, on purpose offboarding.

I checked back in with CEO Amanda Lannert to find out how it works in a 100 percent virtual environment, which is how Jellyvision currently conducts business.

Graceful leave is still very much a pillar of the company and is now understood as a philosophy that grounds the company. As Lannert shared, "My general counsel has been in the company for 23 years and just gave me over a year of notice. Now it's like a four-month working transition of getting everything out of his brain and out of his paper files into our systems. And it's just so doable." But what if this person suddenly had a change of heart? Well, they don't call it grace for nothing. As Lannert told me, "You're allowed to change your mind."[22]

Lannert told me a story about an employee who left à la graceful leave, though not at the very beginning of her tenure, but still with plenty of time for a replacement to be found. "We just had it used by an executive woman who after the pandemic just really wanted to be with her one-year-old child. She gave a three-month notice saying, 'I'm leaving.' And I asked, 'Why are you leaving?' And she said, 'I need to be with my son.' I asked, 'How much do you need to be with your son?'"[23]

Because the employee gave Lannert a three-month heads-up, she was able to pivot to become a two-day-a-week contractor rather than leave the company altogether. She could keep her toe in the water, and Jellyvision was able to maintain this employee's experience and institutional knowledge.

Delighted with the new arrangement, the woman said, "It never occurred to me."

I understand why such a policy or philosophy wouldn't occur to most leaders. For starters, it's asking a lot of managers. As Lannert reflected, "You say, I'm looking to leave. It is very easy for you to expect your manager, who's just trying to get through a busy month, to move on and say you're not allowed to change your mind." Imagine the trust that's required for an employee to share their process like this with their manager and "believe that they will not be retaliatory." And then, "What if you take the interview, you hate the company and your manager's like, you're not loyal and committed anymore." And finally, it can be a little . . . awkward . . . to be on your way out, but still be at work. Lannert made me laugh when she said, "It's like, you told me my baby's ugly, but you still wanna babysit. . . . It's like, you're not that into me, but we're still dating."[24]

Is this graceful leave practice a self-fulfilling prophecy, a good way to plan, or a philosophy of mutual trust and respect? Regardless of how you see it, one thing is certain: at Jellyvision, they address the elephant in the room (or on the Zoom), and start as they mean to move on.

Rackspace Technology shares this "the end is not the end" philosophy. According to PJ Lovejoy, senior manager of experience and HR communications at Rackspace, thinking about the end at the beginning was something that cofounder and former CEO Graham Weston did from the early days. Apparently, Weston was fond of saying, "Everyone has a last day at Rackspace." As Lovejoy explained, "For whatever reason . . . you retire from Rackspace, or you start something new, or Rackspace sells off your part of the business to another company." Everyone's time at Rackspace must come to an end. Which is why, wisely, "Every Racker is aware that there's something next. So from the beginning, [we ask,] what do I get from being a Racker that is helping to build me for what's next?"[25]

Just because this makes such good sense, however, don't mistake such wisdom for ease. As Lovejoy shared with me, "Of course we want our top talent to stick around, help us drive results." Of course! So, the question becomes, "What can we do while you're here to get the best out of you to give the best to our customers and to one another?" Which brings us right back to one of my favorite topics, and the focus of Chapter Five: "We focus a lot on learning and development."

This is exactly what every smart company should do—regardless of how you conceive of your offboarding. Development, growth, and purpose are the fuel of the Retention Revolution. Smart leaders will support their employees, no strings attached.

As Lovejoy told me, "We focus a lot on career growth opportunities, you know, stretch assignments, to really give Rackers this sense that . . . working at Rackspace, I'm gonna get exposure to so much work that I may not get somewhere else." And Lovejoy should know—he's a boomerang himself. He left Rackspace for a two-year stint at Whataburger, but then decided to return to Rackspace, which brilliantly has a bridging tenure policy, meaning, as Lovejoy shared with me, "If you leave and come back, you maintain your tenure. So I'm technically a five-year Racker, even though I've only been back for one year. I got my five-year flag in December, which was aligned to my original service."[26]

And as a parting gift, Whataburger—as a shining example of retention-revolutionary sportspersonship—gave Lovejoy a boomerang to take with him.

Make It Personal

One of the most important aspects of any job is the sense of personal connection and camaraderie it brings. And one of the reasons people stay at their job is because of their relationships. So, while it's often sad to leave a position, offering ways to stay connected is a wonderful way to keep people close to each other and the company.

What's Your Next Play with Zapier

Imagine you tell your employer you're looking for something new, so you change your LinkedIn profile banner to "open to work." Then, you're swiftly fired and replaced. That's exactly what Bonnie Dilber, recruitment manager at Zapier, read in a post on LinkedIn.[27]

The fact is that everyone (or almost everyone) will have a next job at some point in their career. Companies can pretend this is not the case, which often leads to skulking around and hard feelings, or companies can support all kinds of mobility, even if the employees' next play is somewhere else.

Enter Zapier's Next Play Program, which is designed to normalize these uncomfortable conversations. The Next Play Program supports any employee in their internal (which you read about in Chapter Five) or external job search. According to the Zapier blog, "Yes, this might mean that we help some people plan out their exit strategy. But we're ok with that." Because as they see it, "We think it will help us to retain our people in the long run. It will open the door to more honest conversations across teams, help us plan for attrition, and support our people to go further faster. And it will make Zapier a better place to work."[28] No doubt!

Here's how it works: Those looking for a role outside of Zapier can first connect with their team's people business manager. Then, the employee is paired with two recruiting managers, who will listen to the employee's career interests and, where possible, recommend specific companies or Zapier alums with whom to speak. And, seriously, hold on to your hats . . . the recruiters will also help them prepare by reviewing the employee's résumé and conducting mock interviews.

As Dilber shared on a recent LinkedIn post, "Job transitions are a natural and normal part of working, and it's also normal for early career professionals to transition every few years. This is how we grow, gain new experiences, and increase compensation."[29]

Do these people get it or what?

Dilber continues by underscoring that when it comes to the growth and development of companies' workforces, "Sometimes, that's going to mean they leave your company and true commitment to the growth of your people means supporting that, too." Dilber knows that treating offboarding employees well—a.k.a. embracing the virtuous cycle—is a long-game strategy. Not only does it utilize the talent acquisition team's skills in other ways (hello, secondment!) but, "Imagine leveraging your current employees to help onboard and train their replacements or someone leaving for a few years to gain new skills and then bringing that back to you because they felt so supported every step of the way, even when it meant a transition out of the company!"[30]

And if you can't yet imagine what it would be like to support your exiting employees, now is the perfect time to try.

Investing in Relationships at Lattice

When Cara Allamano, Lattice chief people officer, told her former colleagues at Udemy that she was joining Lattice, they responded, "Isn't that the company that pays people to leave to start their own business? I just don't get how this works."[31]

Yes, it's true. Lattice supports entrepreneurial employees who are ready to leave Lattice and start their own adventure, regardless of what that adventure entails. Lattice acts as first venture capital into the business. Alia Le Cam, global director of communications and public relations, shared that her first boss, Lattice's former vice president of marketing, took advantage of the fund. "He loved the startup world, had an idea for a product, had been at Lattice for four to five years, and was ready to spread his wings and start his own company." Lattice provided $100,000 to help him make his vision come to life. For Le Cam, "It's been a fun way for us as Latticians on the front lines to not only feel like we're giving back to each other and supporting our colleagues as they grow and evolve into what they really want to do, but also to be investors and cheer them on from the sidelines."[32]

Allamano shared about the fund:

> *As the chief people officer who is trying to make the case that we are committed to people's growth, it's really a great way to point to the fact that we're practicing what we preach. And even when our CEO is bidding farewell, he says, "The best case scenario here is that you come back and be part of our fund, and you can help make the world a better place from what you learned here."*[33]

Talk about a shift in perspective!
It's radical. It's revolutionary.

The Revolving Door of Alumni Opportunity

The Chief Learning Officer of Udemy, Melissa Daimler, was in the airport security line at New York's JFK when she was taken with a woman's employee swag—a hat, a jacket, and a backpack with her company's logo. Daimler struck up a conversation with her, and the woman "excitedly told me about it and different roles she played there. That is powerful brand marketing—and it was free."

That's a pretty great reminder of how important employees are as brand ambassadors. But as Daimler put it, "Here is the funny part—she no longer even worked at that company."[34]

So, the next time you think it won't matter how you treat someone as they walk out the door, think of this story. The very best way to offboard as you mean to go on is to establish a rich network of relationships via alumni opportunities. Keeping your former employees connected in some way is good for people *and* good for business.

Alumni may become customers, suppliers, boomerang employees, mentors to current workers, and ambassadors for the brand. A 2022 report from the people analytics firm Visier found that about one-third of external hires are boomerang employees.[35]

And, if you don't create an opportunity for people to stay connected, they'll do it on their own. And you're out of the loop.

Check this out: LinkedIn currently hosts more than 118,000 corporate alumni groups, though most have no formal relationship with their alma mater firms. The result is that many former colleagues connect in groups that are outside the control of the organization they once worked for. Talk about leaving opportunity on the table!

Companies will lose the opportunity to share firm updates, new roles that could be perfect for someone who already knows the inner workings of the company and culture, and, of course, stay in touch with people who could become future clients and customers.

Not to mention, it's good for recruiting new talent. An alumni management software company, PeoplePath, discovered that all the Fortune 1000 companies with formal alumni programs have higher ratings on job search site Glassdoor. Seventeen percent higher than the average, in fact.[36]

And, like everything else in the Retention Revolution, benefits shouldn't be held up like a carrot of attainment, but offered from day one. For instance, McKinsey signs people up for the alumni network on their first day of work, which sends a strong message that you will always be part of this community, even after you leave.

Jenifer Andrasko, executive vice president and global head of alumni at Bain & Company Inc., spoke with *Harvard Business Review* about the importance of normalizing leaving at the beginning, or even sooner. "It actually has to start at recruitment," according to Andrasko. Why would you want to pour precious resources into employees who have left the company? Because, as she says, "They are your talent brand in the marketplace." She continues: "The way that we think about our alumni at Bain is that they are an invaluable part of the Bain ecosystem in creating an engaged promoter base. We have this life cycle–based approach to alumni engagement . . . you need to be talking about your alumni and their successes and the work that they're doing out in the world when you are meeting with recruits."[37]

One of the most robust offboarding experiences and alumni programs comes from one of my favorite human companies, Microsoft. I spoke with Rich Kaplan, board trustee and executive sponsor of the Microsoft Alumni Network, a "group of more than 48,000 plus of the world's most incredible philanthropists, inventors, small business owners, and CEOs working together to make the world a better place." When someone decides to part ways with Microsoft, for whatever reason, there's one clear directive, "No matter how someone leaves, you treat them with respect."[38]

So how does it work? Kaplan sends an email to every person who leaves Microsoft, inviting them to join the alumni network. The email opens: "As you leave the company, you join a new community—the Microsoft alumni community." Pretty radical, huh? It continues, "The Microsoft Alumni Network is the cornerstone of this global community of entrepreneurs, technology startup leaders, business owners, and inspiring nonprofit volunteers."

Who wouldn't want to be a part of that?

Kaplan shared some of the many, meaningful emails he gets back:

> I have worked for multiple organizations and I have never received a note quite like this. Although my time with the organization did not work out, I left knowing this is a great company. Thank you again for your continued success.

> Rich, what a wonderful mail. I have to admit I'm missing my Microsoft family, but excited to share all I learned at Microsoft with the next generation of leaders. Thankful to be part of the community.[39]

The first year of being in the network is free; after that, there are nominal yearly dues. According to Kaplan, there is an 80 percent retention rate after the first year, a mighty enviable number by any measure!

So, what makes this alumni network so successful? Kaplan shared some of the many ways Microsoft keeps employees connected to each other, to Microsoft, and to its values, which—no surprise here—boils down to taking off-boarding very personally. As Kaplan told me: "The key is that the programs are designed with the alumni in the center."[40]

Here are some elements of the program, named after the color of the Microsoft ID, iconic among those who work there, which you can use for some inspiration. As you think about your own alumni opportunities, a fun thing to think about is, What makes your employees easily identifiable?

- ***Beyond the Blue Badge* podcast.** This podcast features (primarily) former employees who talk about key learnings in their career.
- **Alumni bookshelf.** The network is given access to books that former employees have written.
- **AlumConnect.** A place where someone can post a classified ad ("I'm starting a new business and looking for web dev"), ask for recommendations on anything from the personal to the professional, and connect with fellow alumni.
- **Quarterly newsletter.** Written by current executives to the alumni network.
- **Road to Rehire program.** Microsoft receives millions of applications, and recruiters can't always respond to every email, but the alumni network has a dedicated recruiter that responds to every alumnus reapplying to the company.

- **Ongoing learning and development.** If Microsoft is hosting a learning event for employees and it's not full, they often open it up to the alumni network, too.
- **Recruiting fair.** This fair focuses on the value proposition for alumni. Yes, Microsoft attends, but companies like Nordstrom, Starbucks, Boeing, and so on, come to this fair full of Microsoft alums to recruit them. According to Kaplan, 400 people attended the last fair.
- **Regular meetups and discounts on LinkedIn Business products.**

And if this list isn't enough, there's more.

Microsoft has a strong culture of giving for current employees. Every dollar employees give gets matched up to $15,000! Kaplan shared, "We wanted to carry that legacy of giving into the alumni community, and we do it through the 'Microsoft Alumni for Good Challenge'." In 2021, the Microsoft Alumni Network made $100,000 available in matching gifts for grants to alumnae nonprofits, and 129 different nonprofits received a gift across 29 states. "We want to communicate that you might have practiced this at Microsoft, and we want it to continue." That's a whole lot of goodwill moving through the universe! Especially coming from people who don't even work for you anymore. And it's the perfect example of a virtuous cycle: an employee journey, marked by respect and intention from start to finish, is often a perfect circle.

And others are paying attention. Kaplan shared that "execs from several big companies have reached out asking how Microsoft does this."[41] Who can blame them?

As Kaplan told me (and it makes so much sense), "90% of Fortune 500 companies have Microsoft alumni working for them."[42] At Microsoft, 10 percent of all new hires are boomerangs, and for those who move on to other companies, if they remain connected through the alumni network, they become advocates for Microsoft. They inevitably end up recommending Microsoft products and technology. A win-win all around.

Now, I understand that most companies don't have those kinds of numbers or reach. But what matters isn't the impact, which is relative anyway, but, as with everything else in the Retention Revolution—and this book!—it's all about your intention. If, from the beginning of the employee journey, you consider the end, designed with your values in mind, offboarding will definitely become the new onboarding.

It probably won't come as a surprise that Jellyvision also works hard to keep their alumni connected and hosts regular happy hours. But here's the kicker, as told by Lannert:

For our 10th anniversary we invited everybody who had ever been at Jellyvision. And I was shocked at the number of people who showed up, including people I had parted ways with. There were three people in the room that I had had to fire, and they showed up to celebrate the 10th anniversary [because] we had done it gracefully and compassionately and with a little hindsight, they're like I was miserable, and now I'm happier. I'm in a better fit, and it feels really good. I mean, it's crazy how exceptional our alums are. I think a hundred people showed up and like, 30% didn't work at the company anymore.[43]

Now, that's something to celebrate.

Offboarding Well—Even During Layoffs

Every day (and multiple times a day), LinkedIn posts appear that look something like this: "It's hard for me to believe that after 20 years at [Company], I unexpectedly find out about my last day via an email. What a slap in the face. I wish I could have said goodbye to everyone face to face."

Folks, it doesn't have to be like this. Expert gatherer Priya Parker agrees: "The way we gather matters. How we onboard, how we celebrate, how we gather and how we say goodbye are the markings and manifestations of our values. The 'ease' and 'efficiency' of letting people go is a huge missed opportunity to close well."[44]

We need to close well even—and especially—when times are tough.

One of the companies that I have profiled in all my books (including this one) is LinkedIn. So much of what LinkedIn does is linked to its values, and their offboarding is no exception. One of LinkedIn's values is "Relationships Matter." Their alumni newsletter has a tagline, "Relationships Always Matter—even when you are no longer working at LinkedIn!"

Their first newsletter of 2023 began with: "As you may have heard and/or if you were impacted yourself, we unfortunately had some layoffs at LinkedIn last month. If you are looking to hire any talent acquisition professionals, please check out this amazing list of talent."[45] The newsletter went on to share:

1. Information about their quarterly virtual events for alumni
2. An alumni spotlight highlighting their work
3. Free books that can be redeemed (maybe *The Retention Revolution* will be on the list!)

4. An update on the growth of the alumni network (over 1,100 new alumni joined in three months)

I love how LinkedIn is letting alumni know about great people who are available, and they're showing recently impacted employees that they will continue to support them. In other words, *relationships always matter.* Layoffs are hard all around, but addressing the challenges and the support they plan to provide in this newsletter is an example of a company making an effort to close well.

If you have a network of alumni, it would be wise to stay connected to them. And the best part is, it's not rocket science. It could be something as simple as an email newsletter. And that doesn't have to cost very much either!

In closing, I want to share an amazing expression that cuts to the very heart of the Retention Revolution. In Bengali, the phrase *Ami Aschi* translates roughly as both "goodbye" and "I'll be back."[46] If you're doing offboarding right, employees just might let the door hit them on the way out because they know it's coming right back around.

And so are they.

Keeping employees connected to your company means understanding that coming and going are just different aspects of a long and winding relationship—as part of the workforce, as customers, as brand ambassadors, as friends, as humans.

As people move on in their lives, made better by having worked with you and your organization, everyone's ecosystem of opportunities just grows and grows.

And instead of saying goodbye, they'll say, "Be back soon."

That's a (W)RAP

Retention Action Plan for Offboarding

1. Audit your offboarding program if you have one. And if you don't have one, now is the perfect time to create one. Keep the virtuous cycle of the Retention Revolution in mind as you design it.

2. Remember that your employees are at your company for only a stop in their tour of duty. If their time with your company is characterized by support and empathy, the virtuous cycle will retain them within your company ecosystem—through new client work, referrals, as brand ambassadors, or even perhaps as boomerang employees down the line.

3. Communicate internal opportunities widely. Make it easy for employees to find a new role inside the company rather than outside. Unwanted turnover is expensive!

4. Consider a formal employee alumni program that offers mentorships, conferences, newsletters, networking opportunities, professional development, recruiting fairs, and referrals. This is a great way to build goodwill with former employees and see the virtuous cycle at work.

5. Give grace, get grace. Creating a graceful leave policy (and the mutual trust it requires from everyone) gives both employees and employers the time and space to plan. And you might even discover an alternative arrangement for an employee who thought they wanted to leave.

IT'S NOT YOU.
IT'S NOT ME.
IT'S US.

I n 1995, I graduated with an MBA from the Kellogg Graduate School of Business, and in 1996 I joined the Hay Group, a human resources consulting firm—since acquired by Korn Ferry—as a consultant.

I remember those first few weeks of onboarding fondly: being introduced to all my new colleagues, meeting one-on-one with my boss, going to an after-work happy hour or two. And, of course, I got my shiny, new—probably very heavy by today's standards—laptop and the key to the restroom down the hall.

Not a Zoom screen in sight.

As the years went by, I worked on a variety of projects. I was asked what I wanted to learn and given the opportunity to gain experience across different areas of the firm. Because of my interest in, and love of, sports, I was given the chance to help build a sports HR consulting practice. I led client meetings, learned new skills, and developed myself as a professional— up, down, and sideways. I felt like my managers trusted me, and if I needed to take a day off or work from home, there were no questions asked. Flexibility was baked right in.

And then, after four-ish years, it was time to move on.

When I told my boss I was planning to leave, I was really nervous. And he was not happy. He and a few partners got together and asked, "Is there anything we can do to convince you to stay?"

I thought about it, but the answer was no. I was not leaving for more money. I was not leaving because there weren't growth opportunities. I was leaving because I was ready to do something else. In other words, "It's not you, it's me."

So far, this story is a pretty classic before times tale, right? Employee quits job. Employer feels quit-upon.

Until what happened next.

My boss said that while he was disappointed, the door would always be open. In fact, he said that if I changed my mind, I could always come back. And the best part is that I knew he meant it.

This was no desperate push for retention for retention's sake. Instead, the whole process felt truly personal. While I was clearly a top performer, and he would be affected by my absence, he wasn't trying to lock me in with guilt or a set of golden handcuffs. He wasn't thinking of himself or the firm. And instead of telling me not to let the door hit me on the way out, my boss actually held it open for me as I walked through.

Do you see how my story is evidence that the Retention Revolution is a mindset, not a moment in history?

Since that time over 23 years ago, my boss's gracious red-carpet exit set into motion a virtuous cycle of many robust opportunities. One of my peers from my "Hay days" became a lifelong friend, and we started a successful—and really fun!—business together. A few years ago, a partner with whom I had done a lot of work brought me to Columbia University to deliver a keynote about rituals. My former boss and I share thought leadership about the future of work with each other on a regular basis. And over these decades, I've felt incredibly grateful to join Hay Group reunions—both live and remote—and to have an ever-deeper book of business for referrals, inspiration, and friendship.

Cut to spring of 2022, when I started writing this book because people were quitting their jobs in droves, many without even having another job lined up. People wanted something different, just like I did all those years ago. Because of the dramatic nature of the so-called Great Resignation, employers scrambled to keep employees in their seats.

Now, a year later, in spring 2023, the headlines are filled with layoffs, failed banks, and CEOs putting their feet down and demanding employees return to the office. I know it can look like a tug-of-war—from employees having the power, to employers taking it back. But regardless of which way the pendulum is swinging, from The Great Resignation to The Great Recession, what I saw when I wrote my first book in 2018 and what I continue to see more than ever today, is that creating a human workplace is good for people *and* good for business.

Why?

When it comes down to it, it's actually pretty simple. People want to work with leaders who are intentional about connecting them to a purpose, their colleagues, and the organization. They want leaders who will help them learn, develop, and evolve personally and professionally, and then support them when it's time for them to move on, creating ways to stay connected. That's the ecosystem of opportunity, and it gets us all out of the tug-of-war business and puts employers and employees on the same team.

When I think back to my time at the Hay Group, it's not like they did anything spectacular, innovative, or out of the box. They simply understood that as a valued and valuable employee, I was their most important stakeholder, and they treated me as such. And, I gave 150 percent back in return. We continue to support each other to this day.

Isn't that what we all want? From employees, employers, and everyone in our lives? It's only human to want to live a life of meaning and purpose and connection. When I left the Hay Group, it really was a *me* thing. Since Covid, all too many employers, obsessed with retention, have tried to wrest back control and make it a *them* thing.

It's not you; it's not me.

The Retention Revolution makes one thing crystal clear: We're all in this together.

The Retention Revolution is an *us* thing.

ACKNOWLEDGMENTS

Over the past few years, pretty much everything we knew—or thought we knew—about work has changed. While I didn't feel exactly *ready* to write another book, as a workplace strategist, I knew this was my moment.

While I would never want to go back to March 2020 and the center of the storm that was the Covid-19 pandemic, I also don't want to forget what I saw, how I felt, and especially the positive changes I saw in the workplace and in the humanness of leaders.

As I began having conversations with leaders at companies of all shapes and sizes and across all industries, I knew right away that I couldn't sit on the sidelines as the rules of work were being rewritten and quite frankly, revolutionized.

The Retention Revolution was born out of these conversations and is now the third and—yes—final installment of my Human Workplace trilogy.

First, a thank you to my small but mighty team.

To Bethany Saltman, you had me at hello more than 10 years ago! Thank you for your inner and outer wisdom, your collaboration, and your ability to thread the needle.

To Alexa Clements, you continue to amaze me and add more value and insight with every project we do together. I don't think there is anything you can't do.

Thank you to my agent, Jane Dystel, who kept asking when my new idea was coming, and who continues to support my work and is there for me every step of the way. My editor at McGraw Hill, Donya Dickerson, loved the idea for *The Retention Revolution* right away and worked with me to make it happen. Thank you to the rest of the McGraw Hill team: Jeff Weeks, Pattie Amoroso, Maureen Harper, Jonathan Sperling, Scott Sewell, and Steve Straus.

Thank you to Paul Howalt for designing yet another perfect cover that connects this book to the others you've designed. It's a perfect fit.

To my husband, Jeff. Thank you for not freaking out when I told you that I wanted to write another book and for your ongoing love and encouragement for me to always bring my human to work and to life.

To my children—Julia, Caroline, and Daniel. My hope is that this book will help make the workplace better and more human for you and your generation. As you enter the workforce over the next few years, I am excited to watch how you will find work with purpose, flexibility to allow you to integrate work into other aspects of your lives, and work that inspires you to grow.

I am so proud of all of you.

And finally, to my incredibly loyal human workplace community—thank you for reading my books, coming to all my talks—in real life and virtual—adding your insights in the chats, responding to my newsletters, and spreading the good news.

My human workplace wouldn't be the same without you in it.

NOTES

INTRODUCTION

1. Alice Louise Kassens, Jamila Taylor, and William M. Rodgers III. "Mental Health Crisis during the COVID-19 Pandemic." The Century Foundation, April 26, 2022. https://tcf.org/content/report/mental-health-crisis-covid-19 -pandemic/.
2. Katica Roy. "More than a Million Women Have Left the Workforce. The Fed Needs to Consider Them as It Defines 'Full Employment.'" *Fortune*, September 6, 2022. https:// fortune.com/2022/09/06/women-workforce-fed-rates -consider-full-employment-katica-roy/.
3. Roy, "More than a Million Women."
4. US Bureau of Labor Statistics. "Quits: Total Nonfarm [JTSQUL]." Retrieved from FRED, Federal Reserve Bank of St. Louis, January 26, 2023. https://fred.stlouisfed.org /series/JTSQUL.
5. Ann Kellett. "The Texas A&M Professor Who Predicted 'The Great Resignation.'" Texas A&M Today, February 11, 2022. https://today.tamu.edu/2022/02/11/the-texas -am-professor-who-predicted-the-great-resignation/.
6. Katherine Bindley and Chip Cutter. "Tech Workers Face a New Reality as Talent Wars Turn to Pink Slips." *Wall*

Street Journal, November 11, 2022. https://www.wsj.com /articles/tech-workers-face-new-reality-talent-wars-layoffs -meta-twitter-11668167520.

7. Sarah Chaney Cambon. "As White-Collar Layoffs Rise, Blue-Collar Resilience Faces Test in 2023." *Wall Street Journal*, January 8, 2023. https://www.wsj.com/articles /as-white-collar-layoffs-rise-blue-collar-resilience-faces -test-in-2023-11673132989.

8. Sarah Kessler. "Getting Rid of Remote Work Will Take More Than a Downturn." *New York Times*, January 7, 2023. https://www.nytimes.com/2023/01/07/business /dealbook/remote-work-downturn.html.

9. Claire Ballentine and Charlie Wells. "US Employees Say They're Losing the Upper Hand as Layoffs Mount." Bloomberg, August 23, 2022. https://www.bloomberg .com/news/articles/2022-08-23/will-my-boss-give-me -a-raise-us-workers-see-companies-gaining-upper-hand.

10. "Job Openings and Labor Turnover Summary." US Bureau of Labor Statistics, January 4, 2023. https://www.bls.gov /news.release/jolts.nr0.htm.

11. "The Employment Situation—December 2022." US Bureau of Labor Statistics, January 6, 2023. https://www .bls.gov/news.release/pdf/empsit.pdf.

12. Tripp Mickle. "Tech Layoffs Shock Young Workers. The Older People? Not So Much." *New York Times*, January 20, 2023. https://www.nytimes.com/2023/01/20 /technology/tech-layoffs-millennials-gen-x.html.

13. "Employee Tenure Summary." US Bureau of Labor Statistics, September 22, 2022. https://www.bls.gov/news .release/tenure.nr0.htm.

14. Elsie Boskamp. "21 Crucial Career Change Statistics [2023]: How Often Do People Change Jobs?" Zippia, September 15, 2022. https://www.zippia.com/advice /career-change-statistics/.

15. Maury Gittleman. "The 'Great Resignation' in Perspective." US Bureau of Labor Statistics, July 8, 2022. https://doi.org /10.21916/mlr.2022.20.

16. Jessica Elliott. "Open for Business: What You Need to Know About the Pandemic Startup Wave." CO—, October 19, 2021. https://www.uschamber.com/co/start/startup /pandemic-startup-trends.

17. Elliott, "Open for Business."

18. Annie Lowrey. "The Pandemic Business Boom." *Atlantic*, August 6, 2021. https://www.theatlantic.com/ideas/archive /2021/08/pandemic-business-boom/619674/.

19. Lowrey, "Pandemic Business Boom."

20. Lowrey, "Pandemic Business Boom."

21. Shane McFeely and Ben Wigert. "This Fixable Problem Costs U.S. Businesses $1 Trillion." Gallup, March 13, 2019. https://www.gallup.com/workplace/247391/fixable -problem-costs-businesses-trillion.aspx.

22. Steve Cadigan. *Workquake: Embracing the Aftershocks of COVID-19 to Create a Better Model of Working* (Herndon, VA: Amplify Publishing, 2022), 83.

23. Devin Tomb. "72% of Muse Survey Respondents Experienced 'Shift Shock.'" The Muse, August 30, 2022. https://www.themuse.com/advice/shift-shock-muse-survey -2022.

24. Tomb, "Muse Survey Respondents."

25. Greg Iacurci. "'The War for Talent' Continues. 40% of Recent Job Switchers Are Again Looking for a New Position, Survey Finds." CNBC, April 11, 2022. https:// www.cnbc.com/2022/04/11/40percent-of-job-switchers -already-looking-for-new-positions-survey-finds.html.

26. Kathryn Dill. "These People Who Quit Jobs During the Pandemic Say They Have Regrets." *Wall Street Journal*, April 25, 2022. https://www.wsj.com/articles/some-job -switchers-are-having-second-thoughts-great-resignation -11650663370.

27. Cheryl D'Cruz-Young and Clive Smit. "A People-Powered Solution to Climate Change." Korn Ferry, November 14, 2022. https://www.kornferry.com/insights/featured -topics/people-planet-profit/a-people-powered-solution-to -climate-change.

28. Marcus Erb. "Treating Employees Well Led to Higher Stock Prices During the Pandemic." Great Place To Work, August 5, 2021. https://www.greatplacetowork .com/resources/blog/treating-employees-well-led-to-higher -stock-prices-during-the-pandemic.

29. Ryan Pendell. "The World's $7.8 Trillion Workplace Problem." Gallup, June 14, 2022. https://www.gallup .com/workplace/393497/world-trillion-workplace-problem .aspx.

30. "Gallup's Employee Engagement Survey." Gallup, November 14, 2022. https://www.gallup.com/workplace /356063/gallup-q12-employee-engagement-survey.aspx.

CHAPTER ONE

1. Reid Hoffman, Ben Casnocha, and Chris Yeh. "Tours of Duty: The New Employer-Employee Compact." *Harvard Business Review*, June 2013. https://hbr.org/2013/06/tours -of-duty-the-new-employer-employee-compact.

2. McFeely and Wigert. "This Fixable Problem."

3. "From the Great Resignation to Great Retention: The Case for Perfecting Hybrid Onboarding." Eagle Hill, September 13, 2022. https://www.eaglehillconsulting.com/insights /onboarding-process/.

4. "Glint Study Reveals New Hires with Poor Onboarding Experiences Are Eight Times More Likely to Be Disengaged at Work." Glint, October 18, 2016. https://www.glintinc .com/press/glint-study-reveals-new-hires-poor-onboarding -experiences-eight-times-likely-disengaged-work/.

5. "Microsoft Unveils New Employee Experience Platform— Microsoft Viva—to Help People Thrive at Work." Microsoft, February 4, 2021. https://news.microsoft.com /2021/02/04/microsoft-unveils-new-employee-experience -platform-microsoft-viva-to-help-people-thrive-at-work/.

6. Tom Warren. "Xbox and Windows Fall in Microsoft's $51.9 Billion Quarter." Verge, July 26, 2022. https://www .theverge.com/2022/7/26/23278933/microsoft-q4-2022 -earnings-revenue-cloud-windows-xbox-gaming-surface.

7. Anita Ramaswamy and Alex Wilhelm. "Gusto Raises an Extension Round, Following Faire as Unicorns React to a Changing Market." TechCrunch, May 12, 2022. https://techcrunch.com/2022/05/12/gusto-raises-an-extension-round-following-faire-as-unicorns-react-to-a-changing-market/.

8. "How Gusto Built Scalable Hiring Practices Rooted in Tradition." First Round Review, accessed January 29, 2023. https://review.firstround.com/how-gusto-built-scalable-hiring-practices-rooted-in-tradition.

9. "How Gusto Built Scalable Hiring Practices."

10. JazzHR. "HR's Year in Review: What New Data Reveals About 2021." JazzHR Blog, November 9, 2021. https://www.jazzhr.com/blog/2021-hr-year-in-review/.

11. Jesenia Vargas. "Stax Is the Latest Unicorn Company: News Round Up." Stax Payments, November 22, 2022. https://staxpayments.com/blog/stax-is-the-latest-business-unicorn-news-round-up/.

12. Krystal Little (senior vice president business operations, Stax), in discussion with Erica Keswin, 2022.

13. Manager of employee experience (employee, Stax), in discussion with Erica Keswin, 2022.

14. Manager, Stax interview.

15. Manager, Stax interview.

16. Alok Patel and Stephanie Plowman. "The Increasing Importance of a Best Friend at Work." Gallup, August 17, 2022. https://www.gallup.com/workplace/397058/increasing-importance-best-friend-work.aspx.

17. Patel and Plowman, "Increasing Importance."

18. Luke Brodie (client innovation services lead, Accenture's Canada Innovation Hub), in discussion with Erica Keswin, 2022.

19. Brodie, Accenture interview.

20. Naina Dhingra et al. "Help Your Employees Find Purpose—or Watch Them Leave." McKinsey & Company, April 5, 2021. https://www.mckinsey.com/capabilities/people-and-organizational-performance/our-insights/help-your-employees-find-purpose-or-watch-them-leave.

21. Leena Nair et al. "Use Purpose to Transform Your Workplace." *Harvard Business Review*, February 15, 2022. https://hbr.org/2022/03/use-purpose-to-transform-your-workplace.
22. David Siegel (chief executive officer, Meetup), in discussion with Erica Keswin, 2022.
23. Siegel, Meetup interview.
24. Siegel, Meetup interview.
25. Christy Lake (chief people officer, Twilio), in discussion with Erica Keswin, 2022.
26. Lake, Twilio interview.
27. Sarah Broughton (principal, Rowland+Broughton), in discussion with Erica Keswin, March 2023.
28. Broughton, Rowland+Broughton interview.
29. Adam Grant and Satya Nadella. "Satya Nadella is building the future (Transcript)," May 24, 2022, in *ReThinking with Adam Grant*. Podcast.
30. Daniel Huerta (former demand generation manager, Humu), in discussion with Erica Keswin, 2022.
31. Huerta, Humu interview.
32. Lynn Chikasuye. "6 Tips for Successful Dispersed Onboarding." Humu, March 2, 2022. https://www.humu.com/blog/7-tips-for-successful-dispersed-onboarding.
33. Huerta, Humu interview.
34. Huerta, Humu interview.
35. Kurt Nelson, Tim Houlihan, and Liz Fosslien. "Liz Fosslien: The Smile File," March 4, 2019, in *Behavioral Grooves*. Podcast. https://www.youtube.com/watch?v=qaspp95WbTI.
36. Chikasuye. "Successful Dispersed Onboarding."
37. Sam Forsdick. "Satya Nadella on Why He Has Had to 'Refound' Microsoft." Raconteur, May 25, 2022. https://www.raconteur.net/leadership/satya-nadella-microsoft-refounding/.
38. Forsdick, "Satya Nadella."
39. Joe Whittinghill (corporate vice president, talent, Microsoft), in discussion with Erica Keswin, 2022.

40. Whittinghill, Microsoft interview.
41. Whittinghill, Microsoft interview.
42. Whittinghill, Microsoft interview.
43. Whittinghill, Microsoft interview.

CHAPTER TWO

1. Callum Borchers. "This Summer, the Boss Is in the Office While Employees Hit the Beach." *Wall Street Journal*, August 18, 2022. https://www.wsj.com/articles/this-year-the-boss-is-in-the-office-while-employees-hit-the-beach-11660768833.
2. Ruth Umoh. "The Office of the Future Will Be Intentional About In-Person Work, Cater to Employees, and Driven by Performance Metrics." *Fortune*, December 6, 2022. https://fortune.com/2022/12/06/return-to-office-future-2023-in-person-work-performance-metrics-hybrid/.
3. Jane Thier. "Workers Hate Being in the Office so Much, Many Would Rather Get a Root Canal." *Fortune*, January 16, 2023. https://fortune.com/2023/01/16/workers-prefer-root-canal-over-office-return/.
4. André Dua et al. "Americans Are Embracing Flexible Work—and They Want More of It." McKinsey & Company, June 23, 2022. https://www.mckinsey.com/industries/real-estate/our-insights/americans-are-embracing-flexible-work-and-they-want-more-of-it.
5. Jennifer Liu. "American Workers Aren't Returning to the Office like Their International Counterparts—Here's Why." CNBC, March 2, 2023. https://www.cnbc.com/2023/03/02/why-us-return-to-office-plans-are-lagging-behind-global-cities.html.
6. Dua et al., "Americans Are Embracing Flexible Work."
7. Laura Vanderkam. "Will Half of People Be Working Remotely By 2020?" *Fast Company*, August 14, 2014. https://www.fastcompany.com/3034286/will-half-of-people-be-working-remotely-by-2020.
8. Karen Kaplan. "Want to Keep Top Talent? Create Clear Paths to Advancement." *Fast Company*, September 6,

2022. https://www.fastcompany.com/90782072/want-to -keep-top-talent-create-clear-paths-to-advancement.

9. Kaplan, "Want to Keep Top Talent?"

10. Brian Elliott, Sheela Subramanian, and Helen Kupp. *How the Future Works: Leading Flexible Teams To Do The Best Work of Their Lives* (Hoboken, NJ: Wiley, 2022), 15.

11. Dua et al., "Americans Are Embracing Flexible Work."

12. Bonnie Dowling et al. "Hybrid Work: Making It Fit with Your Diversity, Equity, and Inclusion Strategy." McKinsey & Company, April 20, 2022. https:// www.mckinsey.com/capabilities/people-and-organizational -performance/our-insights/hybrid-work-making-it-fit-with -your-diversity-equity-and-inclusion-strategy.

13. Kaplan, "Want to Keep Top Talent?"

14. Sean N. Woodroffe (senior executive vice president and chief people officer, TIAA), in discussion with Erica Keswin, 2022.

15. Shelley Zalis. "Predictable Flexibility: The Key to Making Post-Pandemic Workplaces Work for Women." *Forbes*, April 14, 2021. https://www.forbes.com/sites/shelleyzalis /2021/04/14/predictable-flexibility-the-key-to-making-post -pandemic-workplaces-work-for-women/.

16. Dua et al., "Americans Are Embracing Flexible Work."

17. Rebecca Johannsen and Paul J. Zak. "Autonomy Raises Productivity: An Experiment Measuring Neurophysiology." *Frontiers in Psychology*, vol. 11, May 15, 2020. https://doi .org/10.3389/fpsyg.2020.00963.

18. Deborah Lovich. "If Employers Would Measure Performance, Rather than Showing Up, There Wouldn't Be a Market for 'Mouse Jigglers.'" *Forbes*, September 7, 2022. https://www.forbes.com/sites/deborahlovich/2022 /09/07/if-employers-would-measure-performance-rather -than-showing-up-there-wouldnt-be-a-market-for-mouse -jigglers/.

19. Jena McGregor. "Microsoft Says 'Productivity Paranoia' Can Hurt Hybrid Workplaces." *Forbes*, September 22,

2022.   https://www.forbes.com/sites/jenamcgregor/2022
/09/22/microsoft-says-productivity-paranoia-can-hurt
-hybrid-workplaces/?sh=5cab277e3f3a.

20. Rani Molla. "Remote Workers Are Wasting Their Time
Proving They're Actually Working." *Vox*, September 22,
2022. https://www.vox.com/recode/2022/9/22/23360887
/remote-work-productivity-theater-back-to-office.

21. "Great Expectations: Making Hybrid Work *Work*."
Microsoft, March 16, 2022. https://www.microsoft.com
/en-us/worklab/work-trend-index/great-expectations
-making-hybrid-work-work.

22. Alison Beard. "Advice from the CEO of an All-Remote
Company," September 27, 2022 in *HBR IdeaCast*. Podcast.
https://hbr.org/podcast/2022/09/advice-from-the-ceo-of
-an-all-remote-company.

23. Beard, "Advice from the CEO."

24. Colette Stallbaumer (general manager, Microsoft 365
and Future of Work Marketing), in discussion with Erica
Keswin, 2022.

25. Steve Glaveski. "Remote Work Should Be (Mostly)
Asynchronous." *Harvard Business Review*, December
1, 2021. https://hbr.org/2021/12/remote-work-should-be
-mostly-asynchronous.

26. Eric Severson (chief people and belonging officer, Neiman
Marcus Group), in discussion with Erica Keswin, 2022.

27. Severson, Neiman Marcus Group interview.

28. Kevin J. Delaney. "An Inside Look at Harry's Return to
Office Plans." *Charter*, February 28, 2022. https://time
.com/charter/6151881/harrys-hybrid-office-return/.

29. Leslie A. Perlow and Jessica L. Porter. "Making Time Off
Predictable—and Required." *Harvard Business Review*,
October 2009. https://hbr.org/2009/10/making-time-off
-predictable-and-required.

30. Perlow and Porter, "Making Time Off Predictable."

31. Perlow and Porter, "Making Time Off Predictable."

32. Michelle Cheng. "Amazon and Starbucks Are Giving Low-Wage Workers More Job Flexibility." Quartz, November 6, 2021. https://qz.com/2085213/amazon-walmart-and-starbucks-are-offering-flexible-schedules.

33. Cecile Alper-Leroux. "The Case for Giving Hourly Workers Greater Scheduling Flexibility." *Fast Company*, April 30, 2022. https://www.fastcompany.com/90745263/the-case-for-giving-hourly-workers-greater-scheduling-flexibility.

34. Jacqueline Williams-Roll (chief human resources officer, General Mills), in discussion with Erica Keswin, 2022.

35. Julia Dhar et al. "Why Deskless Workers Are Leaving—and How to Win Them Back." BCG, July 7, 2022. https://www.bcg.com/publications/2022/why-deskless-workers-are-leaving-and-how-to-win-them-back.

36. Rob Sadow (chief executive officer and cofounder, Scoop), in discussion with Erica Keswin, February 21, 2023.

37. Jena McGregor. "A New 'Flex Index' Is Collecting Companies' Remote Work Policies in One Searchable Tool." *Forbes*, February 7, 2023. https://www.forbes.com/sites/jenamcgregor/2023/02/07/a-new-flex-index-is-collecting-companies-remote-work-policies-in-one-searchable-tool/.

38. Woodroffe, TIAA interview.

39. "COVID-19 Pandemic Triggers 25% Increase in Prevalence of Anxiety and Depression Worldwide." World Health Organization, March 2, 2022. https://www.who.int/news/item/02-03-2022-covid-19-pandemic-triggers-25-increase-in-prevalence-of-anxiety-and-depression-worldwide.

40. Nirmita Panchal et al. "The Implications of COVID-19 for Mental Health and Substance Use." KFF, February 10, 2021. https://www.kff.org/coronavirus-covid-19/issue-brief/the-implications-of-covid-19-for-mental-health-and-substance-use/.

41. Maddy Savage. "Why the Pandemic Is Causing Spikes in Break-Ups and Divorces." BBC, December 6, 2020. https://www.bbc.com/worklife/article/20201203-why-the-pandemic-is-causing-spikes-in-break-ups-and-divorces.

42. "The Shadow Pandemic: Violence against Women during COVID-19." UN Women, accessed January 29, 2023. https://www.unwomen.org/en/news/in-focus/in-focus -gender-equality-in-covid-19-response/violence-against -women-during-covid-19.

43. Vignesh Ramachandran. "Stanford Researchers Identify Four Causes for 'Zoom Fatigue' and Their Simple Fixes." *Stanford News*, February 23, 2021. https://news.stanford .edu/2021/02/23/four-causes-zoom-fatigue-solutions/.

44. Hayden Brown et al. "Brainstorm Tech 2022: Back to Work—Whenever, Wherever." *Fortune*, July 12, 2022. https://fortune.com/videos/watch/Brainstorm-Tech-2022 -Back-To-Work--Whenever-Wherever/43a4a171-8dca-4c81 -88e7-0059ca103bd9.

45. Umoh, "Office of the Future."

46. Kevin J. Delaney. "How to Make In-Office Time Strengthen Culture and Productivity." *Charter*, January 22, 2023. https://www.charterworks.com/ideo-paul-bennett/.

47. Delaney, "Make In-Office Time Strengthen Culture."

48. Delaney, "Make In-Office Time Strengthen Culture."

49. Erica Keswin. "In the Hybrid Era, On-Sites Are the New Off-Sites." *Harvard Business Review*, January 6, 2022. https://hbr.org/2022/01/in-the-hybrid-era-on-sites-are-the -new-off-sites.

50. Perla Bernstein (chief of staff, EA Markets), in discussion with Erica Keswin, January 31, 2023.

51. Tena Latona (chief executive officer, WITS), in discussion with Erica Keswin, 2022.

52. Patrick Hatton (area vice president of operations, Hyatt), in discussion with Erica Keswin, 2022.

53. Stephanie Braming (global head investment management, William Blair), in discussion with Erica Keswin, 2022.

54. Saffro Charlie (president and founder, CS Recruiting), in discussion with Erica Keswin, 2022.

55. Saffro, CS Recruiting interview.

56. Dowling et al., "Hybrid Work."

57. Elliott et al., *How the Future Works*, 52.

58. Tim Henderson. "As Women Return to Jobs, Remote Work Could Lock in Gains." Pew Charitable Trusts, May 3, 2022. https://www.pewtrusts.org/en/research-and -analysis/blogs/stateline/2022/05/03/as-women-return-to -jobs-remote-work-could-lock-in-gains.

59. Henderson, "As Women Return to Jobs."

60. Stephanie Kramer (chief human resources officer, L'Oréal USA), in discussion with Erica Keswin, 2022.

61. Rachel Pelta. "Survey: Men & Women Experience Remote Work Differently." FlexJobs, December 16, 2022. https:// www.flexjobs.com/blog/post/men-women-experience -remote-work-survey/.

62. Arlene S. Hirsch. "Preventing Proximity Bias in a Hybrid Workplace." SHRM, March 22, 2022. https://www.shrm .org/resourcesandtools/hr-topics/employee-relations/pages /preventing-proximity-bias-in-a-hybrid-workplace.aspx.

63. "Proximity Bias Is Real: 96% of Leaders Notice Employee Contributions More at the Office, Envoy at Work Survey Reveals." Business Wire, September 28, 2022. https:// www.businesswire.com/news/home/20220928005262/en /Proximity-Bias-Is-Real-96-of-Leaders-Notice-Employee -Contributions-More-at-the-Office-Envoy-At-Work -Survey-Reveals.

64. Greg Jericho. "Women Continue to Carry the Load When It Comes to Unpaid Work." *Guardian*, February 22, 2021. https://www.theguardian.com/business/grogonomics/2021 /feb/23/women-continue-to-carry-the-load-when-it-comes -to-unpaid-work.

65. Aimee Picchi. "Women Do More Grunt Work at Home, No Matter Their Pay or Education." CBS News, January 23, 2020. https://www.cbsnews.com/news/women-extra -unpaid-hours-full-time-jobs/.

66. "Leveling the Playing Field in the New Hybrid Workplace." Future Forum, January 25, 2022. https://futureforum.com /2022/01/25/leveling-the-playing-field-in-the-new-hybrid -workplace/.

67. Eve Rodsky (author, *Fair Play*), in discussion with Erica Keswin, 2023.

68. Erin Grau (cofounder, Charter), in discussion with Erica Keswin, February 2023.

69. Grau, Charter interview.

70. Grau, Charter interview.

71. Ben Casselman. "For Disabled Workers, a Tight Labor Market Opens New Doors." *New York Times*, October 25, 2022. https://www.nytimes.com/2022/10/25/business /economy/labor-disabilities.html.

72. Karla L. Miller. "Microaggressions at the Office Can Make Remote Work Even More Appealing." *Washington Post*, May 13, 2021. https://www.washingtonpost.com /business/2021/05/13/workplace-microaggressions-remote -workers/.

73. Joi Childs (@jumpedforjoi). "I feel like we don't talk enough about the benefits of working from home as a person of color. Especially because we have to deal with the micro aggressions that come with 'office culture.'" Twitter, May 7, 2021. https://twitter.com/jumpedforjoi /status/1390721307730354179.

74. Miller, "Microaggressions at the Office."

CHAPTER THREE

1. Adam Grant. "The Not-So-Great Resignation," April 12, 2022, in *WorkLife with Adam Grant*. Podcast. https:// www.ted.com/talks/worklife_with_adam_grant_the_not _so_great_resignation.

2. "Top 50 Influential Neurodivergent Women 2022." Women Beyond the Box, 2022. https://www.womenbeyondthebox .com/50-influencers-2022/.

3. Ellie Middleton. "Can we pls talk for a minute about the outdated idea of what is/isn't 'professional' . . ." post. LinkedIn, October 26, 2021. https://www.linkedin.com /posts/elliemidds_can-we-pls-talk-for-a-minute-about-the -outdated-activity-6858668363242180608-A2xT/.

4. Rani Molla. "Tell Your Boss: Working from Home Is Making You More Productive." *Vox*, May 30, 2022. https://www.vox.com/recode/23129752/work-from-home-productivity.

5. Sunny Bonnell and Ashleigh Hansberger. "7 Reasons Why Emotional Leaders Are the Future." *Fast Company*, July 21, 2022. https://www.fastcompany.com/90770829/7-reasons-why-emotional-leaders-are-the-future.

6. "Professional." Merriam-Webster, accessed January 29, 2023. https://www.merriam-webster.com/.

7. Laura Delizonna. "High-Performing Teams Need Psychological Safety: Here's How to Create It." *Harvard Business Review*, August 24, 2017. https://hbr.org/2017/08/high-performing-teams-need-psychological-safety-heres-how-to-create-it.

8. Cecelia Herbert. "Belonging at Work: The Top Driver of Employee Engagement." Qualtrics, September 16, 2022. https://www.qualtrics.com/blog/belonging-at-work/.

9. Priya Parker. "7 Secrets of a Highly Successful Dress Code." Priya Parker, October 2022. https://mailchi.mp/priyaparker/dress-code-secrets?e=ef289e46e0.

10. Enrica N. Ruggs and Mikki R. Hebl. "Do Employees' Tattoos Leave a Mark on Customers' Reactions to Products and Organizations?" *Journal of Organizational Behavior* 43, no. 6 (2022): 965–82. https://doi.org/10.1002/job.2616.

11. Jo Constantz. "Considering a Tattoo? It May Not Be Bad for Your Career After All." Bloomberg, July 18, 2022. https://www.bloomberg.com/news/articles/2022-07-18/tattoos-in-the-workplace-changing-attitudes-on-how-ink-impacts-your-career.

12. Constantz, "Considering a Tattoo?"

13. Lindsey Pollak. *The Remix: How to Lead and Succeed in the Multigenerational Workplace* (New York, NY: Harper Business, 2019).

14. Khristopher J. Brooks. "For Black Workers, an Unwelcome Workplace Focus on Their Hair." CBS News, December

1, 2020. https://www.cbsnews.com/news/natural-black-hairstyles-workplace-employers/.

15. "California Becomes First State to Ban Discrimination Against Natural Hair." CBS News, July 4, 2019. https://www.cbsnews.com/news/crown-act-california-becomes-first-state-to-ban-discrimination-against-natural-hair/.

16. Zuhairah Washington and Laura Morgan Roberts. "Women of Color Get Less Support at Work. Here's How Managers Can Change That." Harvard Business Review, March 4, 2019. https://hbr.org/2019/03/women-of-color-get-less-support-at-work-heres-how-managers-can-change-that.

17. Richard Thompson Ford. "A Brief History of Dress Codes in the Workplace." Fortune, February 9, 2021. https://fortune.com/longform/office-dress-codes-casual-friday-history-book-excerpt-richard-thompson-ford/.

18. Ford, "Brief History of Dress Codes."

19. McFeely and Wigert. "This Fixable Problem."

20. Debi Yadegari (chief executive officer and founder, Villyge), in discussion with Erica Keswin, 2022.

21. "Villyge Market Research." Villyge, accessed May 18, 2023. https://acrobat.adobe.com/link/review?uri=urn%3Aaaid%3Ascds%3AUS%3Ac117fa49-3f2c-3b95-871e-4ff20d3ac3c5.

22. Emma Goldberg. "When Your Boss Is Crying, but You're the One Being Laid Off." New York Times, August 24, 2022. https://www.nytimes.com/2022/08/24/business/ceo-crying-linkedin-layoffs.html.

23. Kim Parker and Juliana Menasce Horowitz. "Majority of Workers Who Quit a Job in 2021 Cite Low Pay, No Opportunities for Advancement, Feeling Disrespected." Pew Research Center, March 9, 2022. https://www.pewresearch.org/fact-tank/2022/03/09/majority-of-workers-who-quit-a-job-in-2021-cite-low-pay-no-opportunities-for-advancement-feeling-disrespected/.

24. Richard Edelman. "Edelman Trust Barometer: Special Report on Covid-19 Demonstrates Essential Role of the

Private Sector." Edelman, accessed January 29, 2023. https://www.edelman.com/research/edelman-trust-covid -19-demonstrates-essential-role-of-private-sector.

25. Melissa Marshall (vice president, people and organization, Banfield Pet Hospital), in discussion with Erica Keswin, 2022.

26. Dr. Molly McAllister (chief medical officer, Banfield Pet Hospital), in discussion with Erica Keswin, 2022.

27. Donald Knight (chief people officer, Greenhouse), in discussion with Erica Keswin, 2022.

28. Knight, Greenhouse interview.

29. Derrick Hicks. "Red, Yellow, or Green? A Simple Framework to Connect with Your Team." LinkedIn, March 23, 2020. https://www.linkedin.com/pulse /red-yellow-green-simple-framework-connect-your-team -derrick-hicks/.

30. Daisy Auger-Dominguez. "In a recent 1:1 with one of my direct reports" post. LinkedIn, October 2022. https://www.linkedin.com/posts/daisyaugerdominguez _in-a-recent-11-with-one-my-of-my-direct-activity -6992555684722528256-YajR/.

31. Judith Harrison (chief diversity, equity and inclusion officer, Weber Shandwick), in discussion with Erica Keswin, 2022.

32. Ron Carucci. "To Retain Employees, Give Them a Sense of Purpose and Community." *Harvard Business Review*, October 11, 2021. https://hbr.org/2021/10/to-retain -employees-give-them-a-sense-of-purpose-and-community.

CHAPTER FOUR

1. Joe Manna. "Asynchronous Communication: Get More Done & Avoid Burnout." Nextiva, August 26, 2021. https:// www.nextiva.com/blog/asynchronous-communication .html.

2. Nicholas Shiya. "Asynchronous Work Is Changing the Ways We Work." WeWork, June 15, 2022. https://www .wework.com/ideas/research-insights/expert-insights /asynchronous-work-is-changing-the-ways-we-work.

3. Soulaima Gourani. "Why Most Meetings Fail Before They Even Begin." *Forbes*, May 6, 2021. https://www .forbes.com/sites/soulaimagourani/2021/05/06/why-most -meetings-fail-before-they-even-begin/?sh=77852d411096.

4. Erica Keswin. *Bring Your Human to Work: 10 Surefire Ways to Design a Workplace That Is Good for People, Great for Business, and Just Might Change the World* (New York, NY: McGraw Hill, 2018), 63.

5. "Great Expectations: Making Hybrid Work *Work*."

6. Evan DeFilippis et al. "Collaborating During Coronavirus: The Impact of Covid-19 on the Nature of Work." National Bureau of Economic Research, July 2020. https://www .nber.org/system/files/working_papers/w27612/w27612 .pdf.

7. Taneasha White. " 'Zoom Fatigue' Is Real—Here's How to Cope (and Make It Through Your Next Meeting)." Healthline, February 22, 2021. https://www.healthline .com/health/zoom-fatigue#why-it-happens.

8. Sarah Simon. "Zoom Fatigue Is Real. Here's How to Cope." Verywell Health, March 7, 2021. https://www .verywellhealth.com/zoom-fatigue-reasons-and-tips -5115013.

9. Gourani, "Why Most Meetings Fail."

10. Mark Murphy. " 'Meeting Canceled'—2 Words Your Employees Love to See." *Forbes*, May 31, 2022. https:// www.forbes.com/sites/markmurphy/2022/05/31/if-you -want-to-boost-employee-retention-eliminate-some-of -your-meetings/.

11. Kevin M. Kniffin et al. "Eating Together at the Firehouse: How Workplace Commensality Relates to the Performance of Firefighters." *Human Performance* 28, no. 4 (2015): 281–306. https://doi.org/10.1080 /08959285.2015.1021049.

12. Abby Ellin. "New Women's Groups Focus on Generational Mix." *New York Times*, November 10, 2018. https://www .nytimes.com/2018/11/10/style/intergenerational-womens -groups.html.

13. Brynn Michelich (chief of staff, Jellyvision), in discussion with Erica Keswin, 2022.

14. Priya Parker. *The Art of Gathering: How We Meet and Why It Matters* (New York, NY: Riverhead Books, 2020), 17.

15. Amy Bonsall. "3 Types of Meetings—and How to Do Each One Well." *Harvard Business Review*, September 29, 2022. https://hbr.org/2022/09/3-types-of-meetings-and-how-to-do-each-one-well.

16. Jacqueline Williams-Roll (chief human resources officer, General Mills), in discussion with Erica Keswin, 2022.

17. Williams-Roll, General Mills interview.

18. Hayden Brown (chief executive officer, Upwork), in discussion with Erica Keswin, 2022.

19. Brown, Upwork interview.

20. Brown, Upwork interview.

21. Grace Zuncic (chief people and impact officer, Cotopaxi), in discussion with Erica Keswin, 2022.

22. Zuncic, Cotopaxi interview.

23. Marissa Magno (vice president, people and inclusion, Cotopaxi), in discussion with Erica Keswin, 2022.

24. Magno, Cotopaxi interview.

25. Murthy, Dr. Vivek H. "Our Epidemic of Loneliness and Isolation." Edited by Julianne Holt-Lunstad and Susan Golant. US Department of Health and Human Services, 2023. https://www.hhs.gov/sites/default/files/surgeon-general-social-connection-advisory.pdf.

26. State of the Global Workplace: 2022 Report. Gallup. Accessed June 12, 2023. https://www.gallup.com/workplace/349484/state-of-the-global-workplace.aspx.

27. Amanda Lannert (chief executive officer, Jellyvision), in discussion with Erica Keswin, 2022.

28. Lannert, Jellyvision interview.

29. Michelich, Jellyvision interview.

30. Michelich, Jellyvision interview.

31. Michelich, Jellyvision interview.

32. Olga Ramesh (people coordinator, Meetup), in discussion with Erica Keswin, 2022.

33. Harmony Moua. "Why Having Friends at Work Can Help You and Your Team." Chronus, May 3, 2022. https://chronus.com/blog/why-having-friends-at-work-can-help-you-and-your-team.

34. Knight, Greenhouse interview.

35. Knight, Greenhouse interview.

36. Donald Knight. "Endgame: Building a People Team for a New Era of Work." Greenhouse, accessed May 18, 2023. https://www.greenhouse.com/blog/building-a-people-team-for-a-new-era-of-work.

37. Nia Darville (IDEA program manager, Greenhouse), in discussion with Erica Keswin, 2022.

38. Darville, Greenhouse interview.

39. Severson, Neiman Marcus Group interview.

40. Erin Robertson (director of people strategy and analytics, Neiman Marcus Group), in discussion with Erica Keswin, 2022.

41. Severson, Neiman Marcus Group interview.

42. Paolo Confino. "Dropbox Let Employees Work Remotely and Saw Record-High Turnover. Then It Offered In-Person Retreats. Retention Soared." *Fortune*, December 6, 2022. https://fortune.com/2022/12/06/dropbox-virtual-first-model-asynchronous-work-retention-turnover-remote-work/.

43. Confino, "Dropbox Let Employees Work Remotely."

44. Confino, "Dropbox Let Employees Work Remotely."

45. Confino, "Dropbox Let Employees Work Remotely."

46. Aman Kidwai. "Inside Adobe's Founders Tower, a Space Designed for the Future of Work." HR Brew, March 13, 2023. https://www.hr-brew.com/stories/2023/03/13/inside-adobe-s-founders-tower-a-space-designed-for-the-future-of-work.

47. Gloria Chen. "Expanding Adobe's Presence and Commitments to San Jose." *Adobe* (blog), March 8, 2023.

https://main--blog--adobe.hlx.page/en/drafts/kristine
-hamlett-drafts/expanding-adobe-presence-commitments
-san-jose.

48. Chen. "Expanding Adobe's Presence and Commitments to San Jose."

49. Kidwai, "Inside Adobe's Founders Tower."

50. Kidwai, "Inside Adobe's Founders Tower."

51. Peter Economy. "A New Study of 19 Million Meetings Reveals That Meetings Waste More Time Than Ever (But There Is a Solution)." *Inc.*, January 11, 2019. https:// www.inc.com/peter-economy/a-new-study-of-19000000 -meetings-reveals-that-meetings-waste-more-time-than -ever-but-there-is-a-solution.html.

52. Jaleh Rezaei (@jalehr). "We needed a new rhythm. One that generated the same amount of cumulative connection and context, but relied on less frequent in-person time. In other words—one BIG quarterly wave to replace lots of tiny daily waves." Twitter, September 27, 2022. https:// twitter.com/jalehr/status/1574738170121363459.

53. "Introducing Lab82, Adobe's Employee Experience Experimentation Engine." *Adobe* (blog), December 20, 2022. https://blog.adobe.com/en/publish/2022/12/20 /introducing-lab82-adobes-employee-experience -experimentation-engine.

54. Arvind Krishna. "The IBM Work from Home Pledge." LinkedIn, May 2, 2020. https://www.linkedin.com/pulse /i-pledge-support-my-fellow-ibmers-working-from-home -during-krishna/.

55. Lucy Handley. "The Rise of the 15-Minute Meeting—and How to Run One." CNBC, January 25, 2022. https://www .cnbc.com/2022/01/25/the-rise-of-the-15-minute-meeting -and-how-to-run-one.html.

56. Annie Brown. "The Future Of AI-Driven Meeting Technology." *Forbes*, October 4, 2021. https://www.forbes .com/sites/anniebrown/2021/10/04/the-future-of-ai-driven -meeting-technology/.

57. Brown, "AI-Driven Meeting Technology."

58. Matt Martin. "The State of Meetings in 2020." Clockwise, 2020. https://www.getclockwise.com/blog/the-state-of-meetings-in-2020.

CHAPTER FIVE

1. Dart Lindsley. "HR's New Why." Dart Lindsley, July 11, 2021. https://dartlindsley.com/2021/11/07/hrs-new-why/#:~:text=Employees%20are%20not%20inputs%20to,Business%20is%20transformed.

2. Steve Cadigan. *Workquake: Embracing the Aftershocks of COVID-19 to Create a Better Model of Working* (Herndon, VA: Amplify Publishing, 2022), 122.

3. Cadigan, *Workquake*, 121.

4. "Leadership Conference 2022." Wharton Events. The Wharton School, June 7, 2022.

5. Lindsley, "HR's New Why."

6. Mary Baker and Teresa Zuech. "Gartner Recommends Organizations Confront Three Internal Labor Market Inequities to Retain Talent." Gartner, January 27, 2022. https://www.gartner.com/en/newsroom/2022-01-26-gartner-recommends-organizations-confront-three-internal-labor-market-inequities-to-retain-talent.

7. Baker and Zuech, "Gartner Recommends Organizations."

8. "iCIMS 2023 Workforce Report." iCIMS, September 2022. https://www.icims.com/wp-content/uploads/2022/08/iCIMS-2023-Workforce-Report-FINAL.pdf.

9. "Becoming Irresistible: A New Model for Employee Engagement." Deloitte, January 27, 2015. https://www2.deloitte.com/us/en/insights/deloitte-review/issue-16/employee-engagement-strategies.html.

10. Taylor Blake. "4 Reasons Companies Should Focus on Upskilling During the Economic Downturn." Built In, October 4, 2022. https://builtin.com/career-development/4-reasons-keep-learning-development-upskilling-budget.

11. "Good Coaching Will Attract and Retain Your Dream Employees. And We Can Prove It." Terawatt, January 27, 2023. https://terawatt.co/research-program/.

12. Joiselle Cunningham and Angela Jackson. "How Businesses Can Recruit and Develop More Young People of Color." *Harvard Business Review*, October 5, 2020. https://hbr.org/2020/10/how-businesses-can-recruit-and -develop-more-young-people-of-color.

13. "Survey: Professional Development Is Key to Retaining Talent, But People of Color Report Less Access." Cision, July 5, 2022. https://www.prnewswire.com/news-releases /survey-professional-development-is-key-to-retaining -talent-but-people-of-color-report-less-access-301580611 .html.

14. Jonathan Emmett et al. "This Time It's Personal: Shaping the 'New Possible' through Employee Experience." McKinsey & Company, September 30, 2021. https://www .mckinsey.com/capabilities/people-and-organizational -performance/our-insights/this-time-its-personal-shaping -the-new-possible-through-employee-experience.

15. "Chipotle Announces Third Quarter 2022 Results." Chipotle, October 25, 2022. https://ir.chipotle.com/2022 -10-25-CHIPOTLE-ANNOUNCES-THIRD-QUARTER -2022-RESULTS.

16. Daniel Banks (director of global benefits, Chipotle), in discussion with Erica Keswin, 2022.

17. Banks, Chipotle interview.

18. Banks, Chipotle interview.

19. Kamalpreet Badasha. "How Our Talent Thrives Through a Culture of Continuous Learning." Rackspace, February 1, 2022. https://www.rackspace.com/blog/talent-culture -continuous-learning.

20. PJ Lovejoy (senior manager, racker experience and HR communication, Rackspace), in discussion with Erica Keswin, 2022.

21. Daniel Huerta, Stephen Huerta, and Mindi Cox. "91–Mindi Cox (Chief Marketing & People Officer, O.C. Tanner) on Moving from Employee Engagement to Employee Fulfillment," January 23, 2023 in *Modern People Leader: Forward-Thinking HR*. Podcast. https://podcasts.apple .com/us/podcast/91-mindi-cox-chief-marketing-people -officer-o-c-tanner/id1545875052?i=1000596131727.

22. Mindi Cox (chief marketing and people officer, O.C. Tanner), in discussion with Erica Keswin, March 20, 2023.

23. Cox, O.C. Tanner interview.

24. Huerta, Huerta, and Cox. "Mindi Cox."

25. Ben Reuveni (chief executive officer and cofounder, Gloat), in discussion with Erica Keswin, 2023.

26. Aman Kidwai. "Inside Unilever's Program That Allows Employees to Try Out New Jobs and Gig Working Opportunities at the Company." *Business Insider*, May 5, 2021. https://www.businessinsider.com/unilever-program -allowing-employees-try-out-new-jobs-gig-working-2021 -5.

27. Chris Morris. "As Tech Firms Do Massive Layoffs, Chipotle Is Hiring 15,000 People." *Fortune*, January 26, 2023. https://fortune.com/2023/01/26/chipotle-hiring -15000-people/.

28. Ryan Roslansky. "LinkedIn CEO Ryan Roslansky: 'Your Next Best Employee Is Most Likely Your Current Employee.'" *Fortune*, March 20, 2023. https://fortune.com /2023/03/20/linkedin-ceo-ryan-roslansky-best-employee -careers-leadership-tech/.

29. Helen Tupper and Sarah Ellis. "It's Time to Reimagine Employee Retention." *Harvard Business Review*, July 4, 2022. https://hbr.org/2022/07/its-time-to-reimagine -employee-retention.

30. Laine Joelson Cohen (global head of learning and development, human resources, Citigroup), in discussion with Erica Keswin, 2022.

31. Lauren Venoy. "Real Chemistry Reports Strong 21% Growth During First Half of 2022." Real Chemistry, August 31, 2022. https://www.realchemistry.com/article /real-chemistry-reports-strong-21-growth-during-first-half -of-2022.

32. Wendy Carhart (chief communications, culture and purpose officer, Real Chemistry), in discussion with Erica Keswin, 2022.

33. Jennifer Paganelli (president of earned media and integration, Real Chemistry), in discussion with Erica Keswin, 2022.

34. Paganelli, Real Chemistry interview.

35. Paganelli, Real Chemistry interview.

36. Stella Treas and Sid Sijbrandij. "CEO Shadow Program." GitLab, accessed January 30, 2023. https:// about.gitlab.com/handbook/ceo/shadow/#about-the-ceo -shadow-program.

37. Cherie Arabia (vice president, product experience, Comcast), in discussion with Erica Keswin, 2022.

38. Arabia, Comcast interview.

39. Arabia, Comcast interview.

40. Nathan Jun Poekert. "I tell every person that works for me" post. LinkedIn, October 12, 2022. https://www.linkedin .com/posts/nathanpoekert_i-tell-every-person-that-works -for-me-my-activity-6986042337688793088-AlFT.

41. Deborah Lovich (senior partner, BCG), in discussion with Erica Keswin, 2022.

42. Lovich, BCG interview.

43. "Becoming Irresistible."

44. Nina McQueen. "InDay: Investing in Our Employees So They Can Invest in Themselves." LinkedIn, July 29, 2015. https://blog.linkedin.com/2015/07/29/inday-investing-in -our-employees-so-they-can-invest-in-themselves.

45. Erica Keswin. "Rituals for Taking Professional Development Personally." Rituals Roadmap: The Human Way to Transform Everyday Routines into Workplace Magic (New York, NY: McGraw Hill, 2021), 96.

46. Keswin. "Taking Professional Development Personally."
47. Alia Le Cam (global director of communications and public relations, Lattice), in discussion with Erica Keswin, 2022.
48. Cara Allamano (chief people officer, Lattice), in discussion with Erica Keswin, 2022.
49. Allamano, Lattice interview.
50. Phyllis Furman et al. "The Reinvention of Company Culture." LinkedIn, accessed January 30, 2023. https://business.linkedin.com/content/dam/me/business/en-us/talent-solutions-lodestone/body/pdf/global_talent_trends_2022.pdf.
51. "The ROI of Executive Coaching." American University, accessed January 30, 2023. https://www.american.edu/provost/ogps/executive-education/executive-coaching/roi-of-executive-coaching.cfm.
52. "Becoming Irresistible."
53. Tiffany Dufu (chief executive officer and founder, The Cru), in discussion with Erica Keswin, 2022.
54. Laura Mallers (senior director, external reporting and internal controls, Allbirds), in discussion with Erica Keswin, 2022.
55. Mallers, Allbirds interview.
56. Daniel Huerta, Stephen Huerta, and Brandon Sammut. "98–Brandon Sammut (Chief People Officer, Zapier) on Internal Mobility," February 27, 2023 in *Modern People Leader: Forward-Thinking HR*. Podcast. https://podcasts.apple.com/us/podcast/98-brandon-sammut-chief-people-officer-zapier-on-internal/id1545875052?i=1000601939689.
57. "Glossary: Secondment." Thomson Reuters Practical Law, accessed March 30, 2023. https://content.next.westlaw.com/practical-law/document/I0fa00f05ef0811e28578f7ccc38dcbee/Secondment?viewType=FullText&contextData=(sc.Default).

58. Bonnie Dilber. "Secondments at Zapier: Leveraging the Potential of Our Team." Zapier, January 10, 2023. https://zapier.com/blog/secondments-at-zapier/.
59. Huerta, Huerta, and Sammut. "Internal Mobility."
60. Dilber, "Secondments at Zapier."
61. Dilber, "Secondments at Zapier."
62. Brandon Sammut (chief people officer, Zapier), in discussion with Erica Keswin, March 29, 2023.
63. Sammut, Zapier interview.

CHAPTER SIX

1. "State of the American Manager Report." Gallup, October 21, 2015. https://www.gallup.com/services/182216/state-american-manager-report.aspx.
2. Sara Korolevich. "Horrible Bosses: Are American Workers Quitting Their Jobs or Quitting Their Managers?" GoodHire, January 11, 2022. https://www.goodhire.com/resources/articles/horrible-bosses-survey/.
3. Lauren Florko. "The Plight of the Middle Manager." *Psychology Today*, May 20, 2022. https://www.psychologytoday.com/us/blog/people-planet-profits/202205/the-plight-of-the-middle-manager.
4. Jo Constantz. "The Middle Managers Are Not Alright." Bloomberg, October 20, 2022. https://www.bloomberg.com/news/articles/2022-10-20/middle-managers-most-at-risk-of-burnout-in-return-to-office-era.
5. Erin Delmore and Charlotte Gartenberg. "Why Middle Managers Are Feeling the Squeeze and How to Fix It." *Wall Street Journal*, November 1, 2022. https://www.wsj.com/podcasts/as-we-work/why-middle-managers-are-feeling-the-squeeze-and-how-to-fix-it/12efb5a7-69ab-477e-848a-9550d381c8dc.
6. Alex Christian. "How Flexibility Made Managers Miserable." BBC, November 27, 2022. https://www.bbc.com/worklife/article/20221123-how-flexibility-made-managers-miserable.

7. Julia Herbst. "This Is Why No One Wants to Be a Middle Manager Anymore." *Fast Company*, August 11, 2022. https://www.fastcompany.com/90770650/no-one-wants -to-be-a-middle-manager-anymore.

8. Christian, "Flexibility Made Managers Miserable."

9. "Executives Feel the Strain of Leading in the 'New Normal.'" Future Forum, November 21, 2022. https:// futureforum.com/research/pulse-report-fall-2022 -executives-feel-strain-leading-in-new-normal/.

10. Shannon Mullen O'Keefe. "Take Charge of Work Stress Starting with Your Managers." Gallup, May 15, 2019. https://www.gallup.com/workplace/257501/charge-work -stress-starting-managers.aspx.

11. Tracy Brower. "Managers Have Major Impact on Mental Health: How to Lead for Wellbeing." *Forbes*, January 29, 2023. https://www.forbes.com/sites/tracybrower/2023/01 /29/managers-have-major-impact-on-mental-health-how -to-lead-for-wellbeing/?sh=c9edc9b2ec19.

12. Chip Cutter and Kathryn Dill. "The War to Define What Work Looks Like." *Wall Street Journal*, October 22, 2022. https://www.wsj.com/articles/the-war-to-define-what -work-looks-like-11666411221.

13. Cari Romm Nazeer. "How to Give Middle Managers the Support They Need." *Charter*, October 30, 2022. https:// www.charterworks.com/middle-managers-cara-allamano -lattice/.

14. McFeely and Wigert, "This Fixable Problem."

15. Amy Adkins. "Only One in 10 People Possess the Talent to Manage." Gallup, April 13, 2015. https://www.gallup.com /workplace/236579/one-people-possess-talent-manage.aspx.

16. Daniel Huerta and Stephen Huerta. "69–Melissa Werneck (Global Chief People Officer, Kraft Heinz) on 'The Year of the Manager' at Kraft Heinz," July 13, 2022 in *Modern People Leader: Forward-Thinking HR*. Podcast. https:// podcasts.apple.com/us/podcast/69-melissa-werneck -global-chief-people-officer-kraft/id1545875052?i= 1000569799999.

17. Aman Kidwai. "How Kraft Heinz Boosted Manager Support and Training." HR Brew, December 7, 2022. https://www.hr-brew.com/stories/2022/12/07/how-kraft -heinz-boosted-manager-support-and-training.

18. Huerta and Huerta. "Melissa Werneck."

19. Huerta and Huerta. "Melissa Werneck."

20. Kidwai, "Kraft Heinz Boosted Manager Support."

21. Huerta and Huerta. "Melissa Werneck."

22. Richard H. Thaler and Cass R. Sunstein. *Nudge: Improving Decisions Using the Architecture of Choice* (New Haven, CT: Yale University Press, 2008).

23. Liz Fosslien (head of communications and content, Humu), in discussion with Erica Keswin, 2022.

24. Cox, O.C. Tanner interview.

25. Cox, O.C. Tanner interview.

26. Cox, O.C. Tanner interview.

27. Williams-Roll, General Mills interview.

28. Williams-Roll, General Mills interview.

29. Williams-Roll, General Mills interview.

30. McAllister, Banfield Pet Hospital interview.

31. McAllister, Banfield Pet Hospital interview.

32. Klaus Schwab and Satya Nadella. "Davos 2022: Microsoft's Satya Nadella on the Metaverse, Hybrid Work and Leaders' Changing Roles." World Economic Forum, May 25, 2022. https://www.weforum.org/agenda/2022/05 /davos-2022-mtl-satya-nadella-metaverse-hybrid-work/.

33. Schwab and Nadella, "Davos 2022."

34. Whittinghill, Microsoft interview.

35. Whittinghill, Microsoft interview.

36. Brown, Upwork interview.

37. Brown, Upwork interview.

38. Brown, Upwork interview.

39. Brown, Upwork interview.

40. Brown, Upwork interview.

41. "Squarespace Announces Fourth Quarter and Full Year 2021 Financial Results." Squarespace, March 7, 2022.

https://investors.squarespace.com/news-events-financials
/investor-news/news-details/2022/Squarespace-Announces
-Fourth-Quarter-and-Full-Year-2021-Financial-Results
/default.aspx.

42. Andrew Stern (talent and organizational development, Squarespace), in discussion with Erica Keswin, 2022.

43. Stern, Squarespace interview.

44. Erica Keswin. "To Retain Your Best Employees, Invest in Your Best Managers." *Harvard Business Review*, December 1, 2022. https://hbr.org/2022/12/to-retain-your -best-employees-invest-in-your-best-managers.

CHAPTER SEVEN

1. Joey "La Neve" DeFrancesco. "Joey Quits (Worker Quits Hotel Job with a Marching Band)." YouTube, October 13, 2011. https://www.youtube.com/watch?v= 9A4UGtM4hDQ.

2. James Surowiecki. "Boomerang CEOs Have a Bad Track Record Lately, but Iger's Return Makes Sense for Disney." *Fast Company*, November 23, 2022. https://www .fastcompany.com/90815990/bob-iger-disney-boomerang -ceos.

3. Charlie Wells. " 'Boomerang Employees' Are Going Back to the Old Jobs They Quit." Bloomberg, August 18, 2022. https://www.bloomberg.com/news/articles/2022-08-18 /how-to-quit-some-employees-are-leaving-new-jobs-to-go -back-to-old-ones.

4. John D. Arnold et al. "Welcome Back? Job Performance and Turnover of Boomerang Employees Compared to Internal and External Hires." *Journal of Management* 47, no. 8 (2020): 2198–2225. https://doi.org/10.1177 /0149206320936335.

5. Anthony C. Klotz et al. "The Promise (and Risk) of Boomerang Employees." *Harvard Business Review*, March 15, 2023. https://hbr.org/2023/03/the-promise-and-risk-of -boomerang-employees.

6. Klotz et al., "Promise (and Risk)."
7. Klotz et al., "Promise (and Risk)."
8. Amy Spurling (chief executive officer and founder, Compt), in discussion with Erica Keswin, 2022.
9. Laura Coccaro. "Leaders, You Have a Huge Opportunity with Boomerang Employees. Here's How to Succeed." *Fast Company*, August 3, 2022. https://www.fastcompany.com /90775128/boomerang-employees-are-back.
10. Cadigan, *Workquake*, 19.
11. Rebecca Zucker. "Leave the Door Open for Employees to Return to Your Organization." *Harvard Business Review*, April 21, 2022. https://hbr.org/2022/04/leave-the-door -open-for-employees-to-return-to-your-organization.
12. Adam Grant. "Exit interviews are too late to start the conversation about why people are leaving. We should do entry to interviews to find out why they joined—and stay interviews to figure out how to keep them" post. LinkedIn, January 21, 2023. https://www.linkedin.com/feed/update /urn:li:activity:7022676093509738496/.
13. Zucker, "Leave the Door Open."
14. Zucker, "Leave the Door Open."
15. Chiara Wrocinski (chief administrative officer, Kirkland & Ellis LLP), in discussion with Erica Keswin, March 23, 2023.
16. Nell Gluckman. "To Keep Its Lawyers Close, Kirkland Helps Them Leave." ALM, December 21, 2015. https:// www.law.com/americanlawyer/almID/1202745469950/.
17. "CareerLink Coach." CareerLink Coach in Chicago, IL - Kirkland & Ellis, February 21, 2023. https://staffjobsus .kirkland.com/jobs/12134634-careerlink-coach.
18. Wrocinski, Kirkland & Ellis LLP interview.
19. Claire Bushey. "Kirkland & Ellis Embraces Alumni— Current and Future." Crain's Chicago Business, June 15, 2017. https://www.kirkland.com/files/Kirkland-Embraces -Alumni_Crains061517.pdf.

20. Alison M. Dachner and Erin E Makarius. "Turn Departing Employees into Loyal Alumni." *Harvard Business Review*, March 11, 2021. https://hbr.org/2021/03/turn-departing-employees-into-loyal-alumni.

21. "Alumni Network." Accenture, accessed March 30, 2023. https://www.accenture.com/us-en/careers/explore-careers/area-of-interest/alumni-careers.

22. Lannert, Jellyvision interview.

23. Lannert, Jellyvision interview.

24. Lannert, Jellyvision interview.

25. Lovejoy, Rackspace interview.

26. Lovejoy, Rackspace interview.

27. Bonnie Dilber. "I recently saw a post where someone shared that they were open with their employer that they were seeking their next role, and they turned on their 'Open to Work' banner" post. LinkedIn, March 2023. https://www.linkedin.com/posts/bonnie-dilber_i-recently-saw-a-post-where-someone-shared-activity-7040007234461843456-TAZV.

28. "Helping Zapier Teammates Find Their Next Job." Zapier, April 20, 2022. https://zapier.com/blog/helping-zapier-teammates-find-their-next-job/.

29. Dilber, "I recently saw a post."

30. Dilber, "I recently saw a post."

31. Allamano, Lattice interview.

32. Le Cam, Lattice interview.

33. Allamano, Lattice interview.

34. Melissa Daimler. "Throwing my bags onto the airport security conveyor belt at New York City's JFK Airport Terminal 4" post. LinkedIn, April 4, 2023. https://www.linkedin.com/posts/melissadaimler_airportadventures-jfkairport-traveltales-activity-7049015450420072448-ajTv.

35. Andrea Derler et al. "Boomerang Employees Make a Comeback." Visier Insights Report, 2022. https://assets.ctfassets.net/lbgy40h4xfb7/2FD3xYTYoSL4hvCbu SdCMt/abf61b616ac9f450e02e9de90965695f/220705-pdf -insights-boomerang-FINAL.pdf.

36. "The Surprising Impact Former Employees Have On Glassdoor Ratings." PeoplePath, December 21, 2022. https://www.peoplepath.com/blog/the-surprising-impact -former-employees-have-on-glassdoor-ratings/.

37. Zucker, "Leave the Door Open."

38. Rich Kaplan (board trustee, Microsoft), in discussion with Erica Keswin, 2022.

39. Kaplan, Microsoft interview.

40. Kaplan, Microsoft interview.

41. Kaplan, Microsoft interview.

42. Kaplan, Microsoft interview.

43. Lannert, Jellyvision interview.

44. Priya Parker. "The way we gather matters" post. Instagram, February 16, 2023. https://www.instagram .com/p/CouXRSNONBY/.

45. Steve Cadigan. "Virtually every organization today is experiencing increased staff #turnover" post. LinkedIn, March 18, 2023. https://www.linkedin.com/posts/cadigan _turnover-alumni-activity-7042888753157177345-j5Gq.

46. Mike Rocha. "Ami Aschi." Mike Rocha, July 13, 2013. https://mikejrocha.wordpress.com/2013/07/13/ami-aschi/.

INDEX

Accenture:
  alumni platform of, 186–187
  onboarding at, 21–22
ACE flexibility, 40–66
  autonomy in, 41–51
  connection in, 51–59
  equity in, 59–66
  (See also individual elements)
Adaptive gatherings, 98, 99
Adobe, meetings at, 115–116,
  118
Allamano, Cara, 147–148, 157,
  192–193
Allbirds, professional
  development at, 150–151
All-Llamas meetings, 101–102
Allred, Rachel, 110, 111
Alumni programs, 184–187,
  194–201
Amazon.com, autonomy at, 47
American Eagle Outfitters,
  professional development at,
  142–143
Andrasko, Jenifer, 184, 195
Appearance, professional, 74–78
Apple, 178
Arabia, Cherie, 141–142
Arnold, John, 179
The Art of Gathering (Parker),
  74, 97
Asynchronous (async) work, 93

Atlassian, equity at, 60
Attrition, costs of, 79
Auger-Dominguez, Daisy, 85–86
Autonomy:
  at Boston Consulting Group,
    46–47
  in flexible work, 41–51 (See
    also Flexible work)
  at Harry's, 46
  at Neiman Marcus Group,
    44–46
  old idea of, 5
  and productivity paranoia,
    41–44
  at Scoop, 49–51
  for teams, 44–49
"Autonomy Raises Productivity"
  (Johannsen and Zak), 42

Bain & Company Inc., alumni
  program at, 184, 195
Banfield Pet Hospital:
  human professionalism at,
    82–84
  managers at, 165–167
Banks, Daniel, 130–131
Baym, Nancy, 42–43
BCG (See Boston Consulting
  Group)
Bennett, Paul, 53
Bernstein, Perla, 55

BetterUp, 149
Beyond the Blue Badge podcast, 186
Bharadwaj, Anu, 60
Big Feelings (Fosslien and Duffy), 81
Blake, Taylor, 127
Bonnell, Sunny, 72
Bonsall, Amy, 98
Boomerang employees, 178–179
   attracting, 180 (*See also* Offboarding)
   CEOs as, 178
   ex-employees as, 4, 194
   as "new hires," 7, 179, 199
   reasons for returning, 179–180
Booz Allen Hamilton, 186
Boston Consulting Group (BCG):
   autonomy at, 46–47
   professional development at, 144–145
Braming, Stephanie, 57
Brand ambassadors, ex-employees as, 4, 181
Bravely, 149
Bring Your Human to Work (Keswin), 38, 80, 94, 187
Brodie, Luke, 21–22
Broughton, Sarah, 25–27
Brown, Hayden, 100–101, 169–170
Business case, for professional development, 127–129

Cadigan, Steve, 4, 125, 181
Career Pathways program, 153
CareerLink program, 185
Carhart, Wendy, 138
CEO Shadow program, 140–141
Champions Awards, 164–165
Change, 7–8
   accepting, 4–5
   dynamic, 2, 8–9
Charter, equity at, 63–64
Childers, Katie, 46
Childs, Joi, 65
Chipotle:
   hiring from within at, 136

   professional development at, 129–131
Citigroup, professional development at, 137–138
Clients, ex-employees as, 181
Clifton, Jim, 157
CNBC, 37
Coaching, 148–149, 160
Coccaro, Laura, 180
Cohen, Laine Joelson, 137
Collective, 98
Color psychology, 115–116
Comcast, professional development at, 141–142
Communications, culture, and purpose role, 138–140
Compt, 10
Conference board, 128
Connect Up meetings, 100–101
Connection:
   at CS Recruiting, 58–59
   at EA Markets, 54–55
   with flexible work, 51–59
   with former employees, 186–187
   at Hyatt, 56–57
   at IDEO, 53
   manager check-ins with employees, 82–87
   in meetings, 103–104
   in offboarding, 190–199
   in onboarding, 27–31
   in professional development, 148–151
   Spaghetti Project for, 96–97
   technologies for (*See* Technology)
   through alumni groups, 184–187, 194–201
   through onboarding, 20
   through Villyge, 78–80
   through Working in the Schools, 55–57
   at William Blair, 57–58
Cotopaxi, meetings at, 101–103
Covid-19 pandemic, ix–xi, 3, 8
   check-ins resulting from, 82
   negative situations triggered by, 51–52

obsession with retention
   following, 206
onboarding during, 14
and opportunities for
   flexibility, 38–39
unpaid labor during, 62
Cox, Mindi, 132–133, 162–163
Creative destruction, 3
The Cru, 149–150
CS Recruiting, connection at,
   58–59
Cuddy, Amy, 6
Culture conversations, 32–33
Curious Cardinals, 150
Customers, employees as,
   124–125

Daimler, Melissa, 194
Daniels, Reuben, 54
Darville, Nia, 111, 112
DEI (See Diversity, equity, and
   inclusion)
Delaney, Kevin, 53, 63
Deloitte, 178–179
Destruction, creative, 3
Deutsche Bank AG, 178–179
Dilber, Bonnie, 152, 191, 192
Disabled people, equity for, 65
Disney, 178
Diversity, equity, and inclusion
   (DEI), 6, 128 (See also
   Equity)
Dress code, 74–78
Dress Codes (Ford), 77–78
Dropbox:
   connection role at, 106
   flexible work at, 114–115
   meetings at, 113–115
Duffy, Mollie West, 81
Dufu, Tiffany, 149–150
Dynamic change, 2, 8–9

EA Markets (EA), connection at,
   54–55
Economic Innovation Group
   (EIG), 3
Economic insecurity, xii
Ek, Daniel, 126
EL (Engaging Leader), 163–165

Ellis, Sarah, 137
Emotions at work, 82–87
Employee resource groups
   (ERGs), 150
Employees:
   boomerang (See Boomerang
      employees)
   check-ins with, 82–87
   as customers, 124–125
   flexible work preferred by, 39
   reasons for leaving given by,
      81–82
Employment, average tenure
   in, 2
Engaging Leader (EL), 163–165
Entrepreneurs fund, 193
Entry interviews, 182
Equity, 59–66
   at Atlassian, 60
   at Charter, 63–64
   for disabled people, 65
   Fair Play method for, 63
   gender, 60–63
   at L'Oréal USA, 61
   for people of color and
      marginalized groups, 65
   relative vs. absolute, 60
   and unpaid labor tasks, 62–63
ERGs (employee resource
   groups), 150
Ex-employees, value of, 4, 181,
   182, 194
Exit strategies (See Offboarding)
Experience Hub, 137–138
Expressing feelings, 82–87
EY, 178–179

Fair Play (Rodsky), 41, 62
Fair Play method, 63
Feelings, expressing, 80–87
52+ Learning Hours, 131
First Sip ritual, 176–177
Fisher, Eileen, 118
Flexible work, 9, 35–67
   ACEing, 40–66 (See also ACE
      flexibility)
   at Amazon.com, 47
   at Atlassian, 60
   autonomy in, 41–51

Flexible work (*continued*)
  at Boston Consulting Group,
      46–47
  at Charter, 63–64
  connection in, 51–59
  at CS Recruiting, 58–59
  at Dropbox, 114–115
  at EA Markets, 54–55
  equity in, 59–66
  at General Mills, 47–49
  at Harry's, 46
  at Hyatt, 56–57
  at L'Oréal USA, 61
  at Neiman Marcus Group,
      44–46
  old idea of, 5
  Retention Action Plan for, 67
  Scoop for, 49–51
  at Starbucks, 47
  at TIAA, 40–41
  at Walmart, 47
  at William Blair, 57–58
  and Working in the Schools,
      55–57
Ford, Richard Thompson, 77–78
Fosslien, Liz, 81, 161–162

Gather@s, 110–112
Gattaca plc, 179
Gender equity, 60–63
General Mills:
  autonomy at, 47–49
  managers at, 163–165
  meetings at, 99–100
Generational onboarding, 25–27
GitLab:
  as asynchronous company, 93
  productivity at, 43
  professional development at,
      140–141
Glassdoor, 194
Glaveski, Steve, 44
Gloat, 134–135
Google:
  people experience at, 124
  Project Oxygen, 160
Gottlieb, Harry Nathan, 108, 187
Gourani, Soulaima, 93–94
"Graceful leaving," 187–189

Grant, Adam:
  on exit interviews, 182
  on languishing, 9
  podcast of, 27–28, 70
Grau, Erin, 63–64
Great Place To Work, 9
The Great Recession, 206
The Great Resignation, xi, 205,
      206
Green, Erica, 85
Greenhouse:
  connection role at, 106
  human professionalism at, 84
  meetings at, 110–112, 117
Gusto, pre-onboarding at, 15–16

Hansberger, Ashleigh, 72
Harrison, Judith, 87–88
Harry's, autonomy at, 46
Harvard Business Review, 128,
      179
Hatton, Patrick, 56–57
Hay Group, 204–206
Hill Holliday, 38
Hoffman, Reid, 13
Houston, Drew, 52
Huddles, 83–84
Huerta, Daniel, 28–31, 132
Huerta, Stephen, 132
Human professionalism, 69–90
  at Banfield Pet Hospital, 82–84
  check-ins with employees, 82–87
  creating inspiring space for,
      73–74
  in dress or appearance, 74–78
  at Greenhouse, 84
  learning and development
      for (*See* Professional
      development)
  of managers, 78–80
  at Mural, 85
  at Reboot, 84–85
  Retention Action Plan for, 90
  successful, 87–89
  at Vice Media, Inc., 85–86
  at Weber Shandwick, 87–89
Humu:
  nudges at, 161–162
  onboarding at, 28–31

Hyatt, connection at, 56–57
Hybrid Program, 139–140
Hybrid work, 36
    managing schedules of,
        105–106
    McKinsey report on, 59–60
    meetings in, 92
    Microsoft's research on, 42–43
    opportunities for, 37
    (See also Flexible work)

IBM:
    meetings at, 118–119
    Reuveni at, 134
iCIMS, 180
IDEO, connection at, 53
Iger, Bob, 178
Impact in Action meetings, 102
"In the Hybrid Era, On-Sites
    Are the New Off-Sites"
    (Keswin), 54
InDay, 145–146
Indiana University (IU) Health,
    75–76
Inside out, professional
    development from the,
    145–153
It's the Manager (Clifton), 157
IU (Indiana University) Health,
    75–76

Janowsky, Sarah, 64
Jellyvision:
    alumni program at, 199
    connection role at, 106
    meetings at, 97, 106–109
    offboarding at, 187–189
Jobs, Steve, 178
Johannsen, Rebecca, 42
Jun Poekert, Nathan, 142–143

Kahneman, Daniel, 181
Kaplan, Karen, 38, 39, 198–199
Kaplan, Rich, 196–197
Kirkland Concierge, 185
Kirkland & Ellis LLP,
    offboarding at, 184–185
Kirschner, Phil, 41
Kivvit, 50

Kniffin, Kevin, 95–96
Knight, Donald, 84, 110, 111
Korn Ferry, 8
Kraft Heinz, managers at,
    159–160
Kramer Stephanie, 61

Laban, Allard, 108
Lake, Christy, 25
Lannert, Amanda, 106–109,
    187–189, 199
Lash, Renee, 48
Latona, Tena, 55–56
Lattice:
    offboarding at, 192–193
    professional development at,
        147–148
Layoffs, offboarding during,
    200–201
Le Cam, Alia, 147, 193
Leach, Penelope, 12
Leave policy, 63–64
Letieri, John, 3
Life Hike meetings, 102
Lindsley, Dart, 124
LinkedIn:
    alumni groups on, 194–195,
        200–201
    boomerang employee posts on,
        178–179
    comments on Grant's post on,
        182–183
    InDay at, 145–146
    offboarding at, 200–201
    oversharing on, 80–81
Little, Krystal, 18, 20
L'Oréal USA, equity at, 61
Lovegrove, Nick, 36–37
Lovejoy, PJ, 131–132, 189–190
Lovich, Deborah, 49, 144–145
Lowrey, Annie, 3
Lyman, Kevin, 126

Magno, Marissa, 102–103
Managers, 155–173
    at Banfield Pet Hospital,
        165–167
    elevating and celebrating,
        158–172

Managers (*continued*)
  employee check-ins with, 41,
    82–87
  at General Mills, 163–165
  and Humu, 161–162
  at Kraft Heinz, 159–160
  at Microsoft, 167–169
  at O.C. Tanner, 162–163
  old idea of, 6
  as reasons for turnover, 156,
    157
  Retention Action Plan for, 173
  at Squarespace, 170–171
  stress and burnout in, 157
  at Upwork, 169–170
Marginalized groups, equity for,
  65
Mars Veterinary Health, 82, 83
Marshall, Melissa, 83
Mayo Clinic, 75–76
McAllister, Molly, 83, 165–166
McKinsey:
  alumni network of, 195
  on hybrid work, 59–60
  offboarding at, 195
  on professional development,
    128
Meetings, 91–121
  at Adobe, 115–116, 118
  connection in, 103–104
  at Cotopaxi, 101–103
  at Dropbox, 113–115
  at General Mills, 99–100
  at Greenhouse, 110–112, 117
  hybrid, 92
  at IBM, 118–119
  at Jellyvision, 97, 106–109
  at Meetup, 109–110
  at Microsoft, 118
  at Neiman Marcus Group,
    112–113
  old idea of, 5
  with PairUp, 103–105
  presence in, 105–116
  protocols in, 116–120
  purpose in, 95–103
  Retention Action Plan for, 121
  Three P's of, 95–120
  types of, 98–99

at Upwork, 100–101
at Zapier, 119
Meetup:
  connection role at, 106
  meetings at, 109–110
  onboarding at, 22–23
Michelich, Brynn, 97, 107–109
Microsoft:
  alumni program at, 186,
    196–199
  hybrid work research by,
    42–43
  leadership meetings at, 118
  managers at, 167–169
  onboarding at, 15, 27–28
  re-onboarding at, 31–33
  on Team meetings, 94
Middleton, Ellie, 70–71, 73
Model Coach Care, 167–169
Modern Health, 149
Modern People Leader podcast,
  28, 132, 133, 151
Molla, Rani, 42
Mural:
  connection using, 21–22
  human professionalism at, 85
Murthy, Vivek, 103
The Muse, 7
Mustache Day, 108–109
Mutiny, 117

Nadella, Satya:
  leadership meetings of, 118
  on managers' role, 167–168
  on personal connections,
    27–28
  on remote onboarding, 15
  in re-onboarding, 31–33
Natural hair discrimination,
  76–77
The Necessary Journey
  (Washington), 172
Neiman Marcus Group (NMG):
  flexible work at, 44–46
  meetings at, 112–113
Neurodiversity, 70–71
New businesses, rise in, 2–3
Next Play Program, 152,
  191–192

Nextiva, 93
NMG (*See* Neiman Marcus Group)
No Hard Feelings (Fosslien and Duffy), 81
Nudges, 161–162

O.C. Tanner:
  managers at, 162–163
  professional development at, 132–133
Offboarding, 175–202
  alumni programs, 184–187, 194–201
  at Bain & Company, 184, 195
  and boomerang employees, 178–180
  at Jellyvision, 187–189, 199
  at Kirkland & Ellis, 184–185
  at Lattice, 192–193
  during layoffs, 200–201
  and LinkedIn alumni groups, 194–195, 200–201
  at McKinsey, 195
  at Microsoft, 196–199
  old idea of, 6
  with PeoplePath, 195
  personal connection in, 190–199
  professionalism in, 183–187
  on purpose, 187–190
  at Rackspace, 189–190
  Retention Action Plan for, 202
  at Starbucks, 177–179
  and staying connected, 186–187
  at Zapier, 191–192
Onboarding, 11–34
  at Accenture, 21–22
  generational, 25–27
  at Gusto, 15–16
  at Humu, 28–31
  at Meetup, 22–23
  old idea of, 5
  personal connections in, 27–31
  pre-onboarding, 15–16, 29
  professional approach to, 17–22
  purposeful, 22–25

remote, 14, 15
  and re-onboarding at Microsoft, 31–33
  Retention Action Plan for, 34
  at Rowland+Broughton, 25–27
  at Starbucks, 176–179
  at Stax, 17–20
  Three P's of, 14–15
  at Twilio, 24–25
One Team, Create Joy, and Get It Done, 19
One Upwork Forum, 169–170
Otake, Vanessa, 135

Paganelli, Jennifer, 138–140
PairUp, 103–105
"Pandemic flux syndrome," 6
Parker, Priya:
  on dress codes, 74
  on gathering, 97, 118
  on layoffs, 200
Peak-end rule theory, 181
People of color:
  equity for, 65
  and natural hair discrimination, 76–77
PeoplePath, 195
Perlow, Leslie A., 46–47
Personalization, 171
Peterson, Ashley, 177
Pollak, Lindsey, 75
Porter, Jessica L., 46–47
Pre-onboarding, 15–16, 29
Presence, in meetings, 105–116
Productivity paranoia, 41–44
Professional development, 123–154
  at Allbirds, 150–151
  at American Eagle Outfitters, 142–143
  at Boston Consulting Group, 144–145
  business case for, 127–129
  at Chipotle, 129–131
  at Citigroup, 137–138
  at Comcast, 141–142
  at The Cru, 149–150
  and customers as employees, 124–125

Professional development
    (*continued*)
    designing, 129–135
    at GitLab, 140–141
    with Gloat, 134–135
    from the inside out, 145–153
    at Lattice, 147–148
    at LinkedIn, 145–146
    at O.C. Tanner, 132–133
    old idea of, 5
    opportunities for, 135–145
    power of personal connections
        for, 148–151
    at Rackspace, 131–132
    at Real Chemistry, 138–140
    Retention Action Plan for,
        154
    at Zapier, 151–153
Professionalism:
    defined, 73
    infused with authenticity (*See*
        Human professionalism)
    in offboarding, 183–187
    old idea of, 5
    in onboarding, 17–22
    unpacking concept of, 73
Profitability, 9
Project Oxygen, 160
Project WIN, 160
Protocols, meeting, 116–120
Psychological safety, 183
Purpose:
    helping employees connect
        with, 4–5
    in meetings, 95–103
    in offboarding, 187–190
    in onboarding, 22–25

Qualtrics:
    on belonging, 73
    connection role at, 106

Rackspace Technology:
    offboarding at, 189–190
    professional development at,
        131–132
Ramesh, Olga, 109
R+B (Rowland+Broughton),
    onboarding at, 25–27

Real Chemistry, professional
    development at, 138–140
Reboot, human professionalism
    at, 84–85
"Red, yellow, green" system,
    84–85
Reeves, Josh, 16
Referral sources, ex-employees
    as, 4, 181, 182
Relational gatherings, 98–99
The Remix (Pollak), 75
Remote work, 36
    home/work lines blurred in,
        71–72
    meetings in, 94
    onboarding in, 14, 15
    opportunities for, 37
    (*See also* Flexible work)
Re-onboarding, 31–33
Retention:
    asking employees about, 32–33
    definition of, 4
    reframing, xiv
Retention Action Plan ([W]RAP):
    for flexible work, 67
    for human professionalism, 90
    for managers, 173
    for meetings, 121
    for offboarding, 202
    for onboarding, 34
    for professional development,
        154
Retention Revolution, xiv, 4
    as an *us* thing, 207
    appreciation of character in,
        74
    boomerang employees in, 180
    career building in, 13
    customers as employees in, 124
    intention in, 199, 206
    managers as MVPs in, 156
    measuring in, 44
    as mindset, 205
    old vs. new ideas in, 5–7
    relative equity in, 60
    success in, 37–38
    virtuous cycle in, 49
Re:Thinking podcast, 27–28
Reuveni, Ben, 134–135

Rezaei, Jaleh, 117
Rituals Roadmap (Keswin),
  19–20, 108, 146, 177
Roberts, Laura Morgan, 77
Robertson, Erin, 113
Rodsky, Eve, 41, 62–63
Roslansky, Ryan, 136
Rothbard, Nancy, 86
Rousseau, Denise, 156–157
Rowland+Broughton (R+B),
  onboarding at, 25–27

Sadow, Rob, 50
Saffro, Charlie, 58, 59
Salerno-Robin, Angela, 88
Sammut, Brandon, 151–153
Scherrman, Molly, 50
Schultz, Howard, 178
Scoop, 49–51
SDT (self-determination theory),
  133
Secondment program, 151–152
Self-determination theory (SDT),
  133
Sembly AI, 119–120
Service providers, ex-employees
  as, 4
Severson, Eric, 44–46, 112, 113
Shiya, Nicholas, 93
Short-term hires, cost of, 3
Shteinberg, Danny, 135
Siegel, David, 23–24, 110
Sijbrandij, Sid, 43
Smile Files, 31
Spaghetti Project, 96–97
Spurling, Amy, 180
Squarespace, managers at,
  170–171
The Squiggly Career (Tupper and
  Ellis), 137
Stability, 2, 8, 9
Stallbaumer, Colette, 43–44
Starbucks:
  autonomy at, 47
  offboarding at, 177–179
  onboarding at, 176–179
Stax, onboarding at, 17–20
Stay interviews, 182
Stern, Andrew, 170–171

Stock prices, 9
Streetman, Rachelle, 131
Summer Camp meetings, 102
Sunstein, Cass R., 161
Superdays, 54–55

Talent, 7
  reconception of, 4
  war for, xiii
Talent velocity, 126
Tattoos, 75–76
Tavis, Anna, 53
Technology:
  beliefs about, 6
  for flexible work, 49–51
  for managers, 161–162
  for meaningful connections,
    103–105
  for meetings, 95–97
  for new employees, 21–22
  for offboarding, 186–187
  for personal development,
    134–135
  for supporting employees,
    78–80
Terawatt, 128
Thaler, Richard H., 161
Thornton, Grant, 7
Three P's of Meetings, 95–120
  Presence, 105–116
  Protocols, 116–120
  Purpose, 95–103
Three P's of Onboarding, 14–15
  Personal, 27–31
  Professional, 17–22
  Purposeful, 22–25
TIAA, 40
Time to Connect, 87–89
Torch, 149
Transactional gatherings, 98
Tupper, Helen, 137
Turnover:
  cost of, 3, 13
  managers as reason for, 156,
    157
  positive return on, 4
  questions to ask about, 9–10
  reasons for, 81–82
Twilio, onboarding at, 24–25

Udemy, 194
Unilever, 135
Unpaid labor, 62–63
Upskilling (*See* Professional development)
Upwork:
  managers at, 169–170
  meetings at, 100–101

Value Conversations, 32
Values:
  engaging managers with, 164
  knowing your, 158
  of Lattice, 147
  offboarding linked to, 200
  onboarding aligned with, 23
  for Superdays, 54
Variety show meetings, 112–113
Vice Media, Inc., human professionalism at, 85–86
Villyge, 78–80

(W)RAP (*See* Retention Action Plan)
Wall Street Journal, 36
Walmart, autonomy at, 47
"War for talent," xiii
Washington, Ella, 172
Washington, Zuhairah, 77
Washington Post, 65
Way of Working (WOW) model, 44–46
Weber Shandwick, human professionalism at, 87–89
Werneck, Melissa, 159–160
Weston, Graham, 189
WeWork, 93
WFH Research project, 71–72
"When Your Boss Is Crying, but You're the One Being Laid Off," 81
Whittinghill, Joe, 32, 33, 168–169
WHO (World Health Organization), 51

William Blair, connection at, 57–58
Williams-Roll, Jacqueline:
  and Engaging Leader program, 163–165
  on flexible work, 47–48
  on remote work, 99, 100
Wisch, Audrey, 150–151
WIT (Working in the Schools), 55–57
Women:
  appearance scrutinization of, 77
  equity for, 60–63
Woodroffe, Sean N., 40, 51
Work:
  asynchronous, 93
  flexible (*See* Flexible work)
  human, 206
  ways of thinking about, 8–10
  (*See also* Hybrid work; Remote work)
Work with Heart, 99–100
Working in the Schools (WIT), 55–57
WorkLife podcast, 70
Workquake (Cadigan), 126, 181
World Health Organization (WHO), 51
WOW (Way of Working) model, 44–46
Wragg, Matthew, 179
Wrocinski, Chiara, 184, 185

Yadegari, Debi, 79

Zak, Paul J., 42
Zapier:
  meetings at, 119
  offboarding at, 191–192
  professional development at, 151–153
Zoom, 52, 96, 97
Zuncic, Grace, 102

ABOUT THE AUTHOR

Photograph by LeshemLoft

Erica Keswin is a bestselling author, internationally sought-after speaker, and workplace strategist. Her first two bestselling books, *Bring Your Human to Work: 10 Surefire Ways to Design a Workplace That's Good for People, Great for Business, and Just Might Change the World* (McGraw Hill, 2018), and *Rituals Roadmap: The Human Way to Transform Everyday Routines into Workplace Magic* (McGraw Hill, 2021) were widely discussed in media outlets like *Good Morning America*, MSNBC, and *Live with Kelly and Ryan*, as well as in many print articles and reviews.

When Erica isn't writing books and offering keynotes, she coaches top-of-the-class businesses, organizations, and individuals to help them improve their performance by honoring relationships in today's hybrid workplace. Erica is honored to be one of Marshall Goldsmith's Top 100 Coaches, as well as one of Business Insider's most innovative coaches. She's also the founder of the Spaghetti Project, a roving ritual devoted to sharing the science and stories of relationships at work. Erica lives in New York City with her husband, Jeff, three children, and her labradoodle, Cruiser.